Quantitative Methods in the Humanities and Social Sciences

Quantitative Methods in the Humanities and Social Sciences is a book series designed to foster research-based conversation with all parts of the university campus – from buildings of ivy-covered stone to technologically savvy walls of glass. Scholarship from international researchers and the esteemed editorial board represents the far-reaching applications of computational analysis, statistical models, computer-based programs, and other quantitative methods. Methods are integrated in a dialogue that is sensitive to the broader context of humanistic study and social science research. Scholars, including among others historians, archaeologists, new media specialists, classicists and linguists, promote this interdisciplinary approach. These texts teach new methodological approaches for contemporary research. Each volume exposes readers to a particular research method. Researchers and students then benefit from exposure to subtleties of the larger project or corpus of work in which the quantitative methods come to fruition.

More information about this series at http://www.springer.com/series/11748

Pascual Cantos-Gómez • Moisés Almela-Sánchez
Editors

Lexical Collocation Analysis

Advances and Applications

Springer

Editors
Pascual Cantos-Gómez
Department of English
University of Murcia
Murcia, Spain

Moisés Almela-Sánchez
Department of English
University of Murcia
Murcia, Spain

ISSN 2199-0956 ISSN 2199-0964 (electronic)
Quantitative Methods in the Humanities and Social Sciences
ISBN 978-3-030-06466-2 ISBN 978-3-319-92582-0 (eBook)
https://doi.org/10.1007/978-3-319-92582-0

Softcover re-print of the Hardcover 1st edition 2018

This Springer imprint is published by the registered company Springer Nature Switzerland AG
The registered company address is: Gewerbestrasse 11, 6330 Cham, Switzerland

Introduction

Borderline phenomena are a fertile ground for scientific inquiry. They stimulate theoretical controversy and open up new opportunities for exploring innovative methodologies. The concept of collocation is illustrative of these possibilities. The special character of collocation, particularly its intermediate position between lexical and grammatical patterning, has favored an integration of perspectives of analysis that in previous stages of linguistics had belonged to separate areas of study. This integration of perspectives is proving fruitful. Six decades after the concept of collocation was introduced – it is attributed to the writings of J. Firth published in the 1950s – the range of topics explored in the literature on collocation and the sophistication of the methods proposed in this field are still far from being exhausted.

Collocational studies are, we dare say, one of the most productive areas of research over the last five decades, judging by the abundance of literature dealing with the topic and by the multiplicity of theoretical insights, methodological frameworks, and practical applications that have resulted from this field of research. The results obtained from collocational research have played a central role in the *lexicalist turn* of the last decades and in the reformulation of the boundaries between vocabulary and grammar. Concepts such as the Sinclairian *idiom principle* or Hoey's *lexical priming* are good epitomes of this tendency. So is the integration of corpus collocation studies and construction grammar, famously initiated by Gries and Stefanowitsch. The fruitfulness of collocational research is further illustrated by the diversity and the effectiveness of practical applications derived from advances in this field. Applied collocational research has produced promising results in various disciplines, including lexicography, second language teaching/learning, and computational linguistics, among others.

It is today beyond question that one of the key factors in the boosting of collocational research has been the incorporation of the new technologies into the tools of linguistic description. As Sinclair envisioned four decades ago, the use of computers and electronic corpora has facilitated the creation of ever more powerful methods of description that, in turn, have made it possible to lay bare forms of lexico-grammatical organization that had remained unnoticed to the unaided observer. This volume lays special emphasis on the coupling of collocational research and computational corpus tools. The common denominator of the papers presented here is the use of computational corpora and quantitative techniques as a means to explore aspects of language patterning that overlap the boundaries between lexis and grammar.

The book opens with a proposal for integrating both collocational and valency phenomena within the overarching theoretical framework of construction grammar. This first chapter, by Thomas Herbst, combines insights from Bybee's usage-based approach to language, from Goldberg's construction grammar, and from Gries and Stefanowitsch's collostructional analysis as a way to account for properties of both collocational patterns and valency patterns.

In Chap. 2, Violeta Seretan makes the case for integrating advances in syntactic parsing and in collocational analysis. After observing that parsing technologies and collocational research have often followed separate paths, Seretan contends that these two areas would benefit mutually from a joint approach to syntactic analysis and to collocation extraction.

Chapter 3 submits an interesting and innovative proposal for complementing corpus data and dictionaries in the identification of specific types of collocations consisting of restricted predicate-argument combinations (*collocates* and *bases*, in Hausmann's terminology). The chapter is authored by Isabel Sánchez-Berriel, Octavio Santana Suárez, Virginia Gutiérrez Rodríguez, and José Pérez Aguiar. As the authors explain, association measures face serious limitations as methods for extracting this type of collocations, which are structurally and semantically more restricted than the Sinclairian node-collocate pair. The strategy proposed by the authors of this chapter for solving this problem is to complement corpus collocational data with network analysis techniques applied to dictionary entries.

In Chap. 4, Vaclav Brezina explains the potential of collocational graphs and networks both as a visualization tool and as an analytical technique. Brezina provides three case studies showing the use of this technique in several areas of descriptive and applied linguistics, particularly in discourse analysis, language learning research, and lexicography.

In Chap. 5, Alexander Wahl and Stefan Gries propose a new, data-driven approach to the identification and extraction of multi-word expressions from corpora. The approach, termed by the acronym MERGE (Multi-word Expressions from the Recursive Grouping of Elements), is based on the selection of bigrams using log-likelihood and their successive combination into larger sequences. The results are validated via human ratings.

Finally, in Chap. 6, Peter Uhrig, Stefan Evert, and Thomas Proisl undertake a thorough analysis and evaluation of factors influencing the performance of collocation extraction methods in parsed corpora. The authors compare the impact of several factors, including parsing scheme, association measure, frequency threshold, type of corpus, and type of collocation. The results of this profound study offer valuable criteria for methodological decisions on collocation extraction.

We would like to conclude this introduction by expressing our gratitude to all the contributors to this volume for having joined us in this project and for helping to make it a reality. A word of gratitude goes also to the referees who have kindly agreed to assist us in the review process, supplying valuable feedback and advice to the authors.

Thanks are also due to Springer's staff Matthew Amboy, Editor Operations Research, for believing in this project and for his assistance and support throughout the preparation of this book, and to Faith Su, Assistant Editor, for her guidance during the production of this volume.

We are confident that this collection can contribute to the development of collocation analysis by providing an interesting illustration of the current trends in this field of research.

Universidad de Murcia, Murcia, Spain

Moisés Almela
Pascual Cantos

Contents

Chapter 1
Is Language a Collostructicon? A Proposal for Looking at Collocations, Valency, Argument Structure and Other Constructions

Thomas Herbst

Abstract This chapter argues in favour of not regarding collocation and valency as strictly discrete categories but rather seeing them as near neighbours in the lexis-grammar continuum. Following Bybee's (Usage-based theory and exemplar representation of constructions. In Hoffmann T, Trousdale G (eds) The Oxford handbook of construction grammar. Oxford University Press, Oxford, pp. 49–69, 2013) analysis of the *drive me crazy* construction, a suggestion will be made for presenting both collocational and valency phenomena in terms of constructions. It will be argued that the constructicon representing speakers' linguistic knowledge contains both item-specific information and generalized information in the form of Goldbergian argument structure constructions (Goldberg 2016) and in particular that the description of valency slots should provide exemplar representations based on the principles of collostructional analysis as developed by Stefanowitsch and Gries (Inter J Coprus Lingusitics 8:209–243, 2003).

1 Why We Know So Much More About Language

1.1 Exciting Times for Linguists

We live in exciting times for linguists. After being dominated by one particular line of thinking for decades with other approaches leading a rather peripheral (!) existence, at least in theoretical linguistics, we now seem to have reached a point where linguists of many different fields who for some reason or other had not been persuaded by the generative enterprise appear to be agreeing on at least a

T. Herbst (✉)
English Linguistics and Interdisciplinary Centre for Research on Lexicography, Valency and Collocation, Friedrich-Alexander-Universität Erlangen-Nürnberg (FAU), Erlangen, Germany
e-mail: thomas.herbst@fau.de

P. Cantos-Gómez, M. Almela-Sánchez (eds.), *Lexical Collocation Analysis*, Quantitative Methods in the Humanities and Social Sciences,
https://doi.org/10.1007/978-3-319-92582-0_1

rough outline of a different framework, which brings together scholars working in cognitive linguistics, corpus linguistics, foreign language acquisition (including lexicography) and also historical linguistics—sailing under labels such as the usage-based approach or construction grammar (Langacker 1987, 2008; Sinclair 2004; Goldberg 1995, 2006; Dąbrowska 2015; Ellis 2003; Lieven 2014; Behrens 2009; Bybee 2010, 2015; Beckner et al. 2009). These developments are largely paralleled and caused by the enormous development in computer technology, as was pointed out by John Sinclair (1991: 1) more than 25 years ago:

> Starved of adequate data, linguistics languished—indeed it became almost introverted. It became fashionable to look inwards to the mind rather than outwards to society. Intuition was the key, and the similarity of language structure to various formal models was emphasized. The communicative role of language was hardly referred to.

Although Sinclair and many other corpus linguists could not be called cognitive linguists, many corpus linguistic insights, especially those concerning multi-word units, collocation and the idiom principle, provide important evidence supporting (and may in some cases have been instrumental in formulating) the position about the nature of language taken in constructionist approaches.

1.2 CxG

It cannot be emphasized too strongly that while not all of the descriptions provided in constructionist frameworks present new insights into the phenomena in question as such, what is worth demonstrating is that these phenomena can be described within this framework, which, after all, is seen by many as offering a more convincing approach towards a comprehensive theory of language than Chomskyan generative linguistics. As most readers will be aware, the fundamental positions proposed in these models include the following[1]:

- Constructionist approaches do not see speakers' linguistic knowledge as being based on inborn properties of the human mind, but envisage it as a network of learned form-meaning pairings called constructions (e.g. Goldberg 2006: 5).[2]
- Constructionist approaches reject a strict dividing line between grammatical and lexical knowledge and work on the assumption of a lexicogrammatical continuum (Langacker 2008: 5).
- Constructionist approaches take linguistic knowledge to be emergent (Bybee 2010: 2).
- Constructionist approaches aim at descriptive adequacy and cognitive plausibility.

[1]Cf. also, for example, Beckner et al. (2009) and Hoffmann and Trousdale (2013: 1–3)

[2]For an outline of the advantages of an approach to language that assumes that knowing a language involves only one type of knowledge, see Stefanowitsch (Stefanowitsch 2011a).

2 Generalizations and Item Specificity

From the point of view of foreign language linguistics, in which phenomena such as collocation and valency (or complementation), which take a position in the centre of the lexicogrammatical continuum assumed by both corpus linguists (Sinclair 2004) and cognitive linguists (Langacker 2008; Goldberg 2006), play a central role, constructionist approaches are an attractive framework because they allow for both item-specific and generalized knowledge to coexist (Goldberg 2006; Bybee 2010), but the role which either plays (for what) is still very much a matter of debate:

> It is as yet not known whether we simply store more and more tokens upon repeated usage, or whether we store more repeated information on a more general and abstract level when available, or whether we do both. (Behrens 2007: 209)

It would indeed be strange to assume that there was no place for generalization in language: Constructionist theories tend to see L1 learning as a process of storage of input and abstraction from it (Bybee 2010; Dąbrowska and Lieven 2005; Lieven 2014; Tomasello 2003). At the same time, it is obvious—and must become clear to language learners at some point of learning a language—that many generalizations do not necessarily apply generally, e.g.:

- Looking at *see*, *bee*, *fee*, etc., one could generalize that words that have a long /iː/ are spelt with a double <ee>; however, looking at *sea*, *tea*, *read*, etc., one could generalize that they are spelt <ea>, and further spellings occur in words such as *key*, *piece*, *be*, *police*, *quay* and *Beauchamp* (Gimson 1989: 101).
- Similarly, *toes*, *foes*, *potatoes* and *tomatoes* allow a generalization of the kind that the grapheme sequence <-oes> is pronounced /əʊz/ in English; but then there is *does* /dʌz/, which, however, makes up 73% of all word-final <-oes>-tokens in the British National Corpus.
- In the area of word formation, we are faced with very much the same sort of situation: *kind* → *kindness*, *great* → *greatness*, *polite* → *politeness* etc., but other adjectives nominalize with {-ity} (*brevity, neutrality*), others take both (*clearness, clarity*), etc.

What this means is that we will have to account for the fact that—in a large number of cases, at least—generalizations cannot replace knowledge about the item in the sense that speakers must know which items belong to a particular generalization. What it does not mean is that generalizations are pointless, because, as a rule, knowing about the various options available for deriving a noun from an adjective will facilitate the learning process when a language learner encounters an established nominalization for the first time.

It is the purpose of this article to take up these issues in the areas of valency and collocation and to explore how a number of cases could be dealt with in a constructionist framework.

3 Argument Structure Constructions: The ITECX View

3.1 Argument Structure Constructions as a Challenge for Valency Theory

Theories of valency or complementation have tended to account for differences such as the ones exemplified by the following examples from the point of view of the verb:

(1) a *Obey the speed limit and* **avoid** *being ticketed.* COCA 2015 NEWS
b ... *she always* **managed** *to get away with it.* COCA 2015 FIC

(2) a *Die Sachen* [accusative] **bearbeitet** *er allein.* DWDS DIE ZEIT 1948 (He is dealing with these matters on his own.)
b ... *auch der Rechnungshof hat sich der Sache* [genitive] **angenommen.** (... the Financial Control Authorities have also attended to the matter.)

Students of Latin were taught that certain verbs *govern* accusative objects and others dative objects; similarly, students learning German must learn whether a verb *takes* a genitive complement (*sich einer Sache annehmen*), an accusative complement (*eine Sache bearbeiten*) or a prepositional complement (*sich an etwas erinnern*) just as learners of English must learn that avoid *has* a valency slot for a V-ing-clause but not for a *to*-infinitive-clause, for example. The metaphors we use to describe the relationship between the verbs and the elements they occur with imply a dominating role of the verb, which, indeed, is the perspective taken in dependency grammars, in particular in valency theory, and, in fact, all other projectionist approaches (Jacobs 2009). The mere fact that information on valency (or complementation) is included in learners' dictionaries or special valency dictionaries shows that they are considered to be related to particular items.[3]

This item-related view was challenged by Goldberg's (1995, 2006) concept of argument structure constructions, which postulates constructions at a high level of abstraction such as the ditransitive and the caused-motion construction (Tables 1.1 and 1.2).

There are two very good reasons to claim that such general constructions exist in the minds of speakers: one is that when speakers are confronted with test sentences such as:

(3) *They meeped him something.*

the majority of speakers will assign some kind of "transfer"-meaning ("intend-CAUSE-RECEIVE") to the invented verb. The other reason is that creative uses occur with verbs used in a construction that speakers will not have experienced before (Goldberg 2006: 73):

[3]When valency or different complementation patterns are dealt with in grammars, they are usually accompanied by lists of verbs that occur in these patterns. See also the pattern grammar approach taken by Francis, Hunston and Manning (Francis et al. 1996; Francis et al. 1998).

Table 1.1 The ditransitive construction (Goldberg 2006: 20)

Sem:	intend-CAUSE- RECEIVE	(agt	rec$_{\text{(secondary topic)}}$	theme)
	verb	(		)
Syn:		Subj	Obj1	Obj2

Table 1.2 The caused-motion cx Goldberg (2006: 41)

Sem:	CAUSE-MOVE	(cause	theme	path/location)
	verb	(		)
Syn:		Subj	Obj1	Obj2

(4) *Pat sneezed the foam off the cappuccino.*

Since Goldberg's (2006) outline of argument structure constructions offers both an explanation of creative language use of the kind demonstrated in (4) and an account of the meaning of constructions, it goes far beyond traditional accounts of verb complementation such as valency theory.

3.2 *Valency as a Challenge for the Theory of Argument Structure Constructions*

There is thus a case for integrating elements of Goldberg's theory of argument structure constructions into e.g. valency theory (Herbst 2011a, Welke 2011; see also Engelberg et al. 2011). However, the opposite is also true, because it is difficult to explain restrictions on the use of particular verbs in particular constructions simply in terms of saying that "the more specific participant role of the verb must

Table 1.3 The English ditransitive construction

AGENT	Action	RECIPIENT	THEME
NP1	Give Tell etc.	NP2	NP3

be construable as an instance of the more general argument role"—Goldberg's (2006: 40) semantic coherence principle. A particularly prominent example of this, so prominent that Goldberg chose it as the title of a book dealing with such restrictions—*Explain Me This*—is the fact that the verb *explain* does not occur in the ditransitive construction in English (whereas *erklären* does in German):

(5) a *The starship explained the physics of resistance fields to her* ... COCA 200 FIC
b ?? *The starship explained her the physics of resistance fields...*

One way of accounting for such restrictions is to supplement the semantic coherence principle by a valency realization principle (Herbst 2011a, 2014ab) to account for the dominating role of stored valency information.[4] However, such a principle is not explicitly required if we assume the items that occur in a construction in established use to be part of the representation of the construction (Goldberg forthcoming). The representation of the ditransitive construction could then take the following form (Table 1.3).

3.3 *Collexemes and ITECXes*

How do we know which verbs are represented in a construction in the minds of speakers? The answer is: we don't. First of all, if we follow the exemplar theory advocated by Bybee (2010), according to which every new language experience changes our knowledge of our language, then the representations speakers have will depend on their individual language experiences. Secondly, we do not know enough about how repeated experience of the same type (say *Person X meets Person Y*) is processed and stored in the brain.

However, it would seem reasonable to assume that the analysis of corpora can at least provide us with some indication of which constructions speakers of a language are likely to have experienced, in what form and how often. Note that this, if applied with sufficient caution, neither ignores differences between individuals nor entails that the mental constructicon be a corpus or like a corpus. But it would be very strange if the analysis of the input would not tell us anything about the nature of the knowledge gained by the input.

[4]See also Boas (2003, 2011), Engelberg et al. (2011), Faulhaber (2011), Herbst (2009, 2010, Herbst 2011a, Herbst 2014a, b), Perek (2015) and Stefanowitsch (2011b). This is why the role of lower-level constructions has been stressed by a number of researchers in cognitive linguistics ("mini-constructions" Boas (2003), Hampe and Schönefeld (2006)).

Table 1.4 Collexemes most strongly attracted to the ditransitive construction (Stefanowitsch and Gries 2003)

Collexeme	Collostruction strength	Collexeme	Collostruction strength
Give (461)	0	Allocate (4)	2.91E-06
Tell (128)	1.6E-127	Wish (9)	3.11E-06
Send (64)	7.26E-68	Accord (3)	8.15E-06
Offer (43)	3.31E-49	Pay (13)	2.34E-05
Show (49)	2.23E-33	Hand (5)	3.01E-05
Cost (20)	1.12E-22	Guarantee (4)	4.72E-05
Teach (15)	4.32E-16	Buy (9)	6.35E-05
Award (7)	1.36E-11	Assign (3)	2.61E-04
Allow (18)	1.12E-10	Charge (4)	3.02E-04
Lend (7)	2.85E-09	Cause (8)	5.56E-04
Deny (8)	4.5E-09	Ask (12)	6.28E-04
Owe (6)	2.67E-08	Afford (4)	1.08E-03
Promise (7)	3.23E-08	Cook (3)	3.34E-03
Earn (7)	2.13E-07	Spare (2)	3.5E-03
Grant (5)	1.33E-06	Drop (3)	2.16E-02

The obvious method to measure the association between a construction and the verbs that occur in it is that of collostructional analysis developed by Stefanowitsch and Gries (2003) (Gries and Stefanowitsch 2004a, b; Stefanowitsch 2014). In their pioneering article outlining the concept of the method, Stefanowitsch and Gries (2003: 214) use the verb slot of the English ditransitive construction to demonstrate that certain lexemes "are strongly attracted or repelled by a particular slot in the construction (i.e. occur more frequently or less frequently than expected)"—lexemes attracted to a construction are called collexemes (Stefanowitsch and Gries 2003: 215). Their analysis, which is based on ICE-GB, identifies the following 30 verbs as showing the highest collostructional strength (Table 1.4).

Stefanowitsch and Gries (2003) use the Fisher-Yates exact test to calculate the probability of an item occurring in a particular construction in a corpus. As in the analysis of collocations, different association measures can be applied, whose characteristics have been discussed widely in the literature (e.g. Evert 2005, 2008, Bartsch 2004, Pecina 2010 or Proisl in preparation).

Fundamental objections to collostructional analysis come from Bybee (2010: 101), who observes[5]:

> lexemes that occur only once in a construction within a corpus are treated in two ways by Collostructional Analysis: if they are frequent throughout the corpus, then they are said to be repelled by the construction and if they are infrequent in the corpus, then they are likely to be attracted to the construction. (Bybee 2010: 101)

[5]Compare also Schmid and Küchenhoff (2013) and Gries (2015). For the influence of frequency and the relevance of different types of frequency measures, see Divjak and Caldwell-Harris (2015).

Whereas, in fact, Gries, Hampe and Schönefeld (Gries et al. 2010: 71) have found that "collostructional strength outperforms frequency as a predictor of speakers' behavior in both production and comprehension tasks", Bybee (2010: 97) argues that "the frequency of the lexeme L in the construction is the most important factor with perhaps the frequency relative to the overall frequency of the construction playing a role". It is for this reason that it may make sense to complement (not replace) collostructional analysis by directional raw frequency data, a method employed by Schmid (2000) in his analysis of shell nouns. I will refer to these as ITECX values ("items-in-construction"; see Goldberg and Herbst in prep.) and distinguish between:

- IT∈CX1, the proportion an item IT makes up of all uses of construction CX (Schmid's 2000: 54 "attraction")
- IT∋CX2, the proportion of the uses of IT in CX as against all uses of IT (Schmid's 2000: 54 "reliance")

ITECX values are thus directional, IT∈CX1 being an illustration of the importance of a particular item for the representation of a construction, IT∋CX2 showing to what extent one can expect an item to occur in a particular construction, which is bound to be a factor relevant to speech processing. Table 1.5 provides the values of collostructional analysis by Stefanowitsch and Gries (2003) with those of an ITECX analysis.

Apart from the fact that ICE-GB seems problematically small to arrive at reliable conclusions in this area since it does not contain ditransitive uses of verbs such as *answer*, *bid*, *book*, *forgive*, *prepare*, etc., the figures for *get* and *do* in Table 1.5, which both have relatively high IT∈CX1- and relatively low IT∋CX2-values (56 and 66 out of 71), show that for certain purposes, it may be more revealing to describe the association between an item and a construction by two separate measures.

4 "It's Constructions All the Way Down": From Argument Structure Constructions to Valency Constructions

The examples of collo-profiles presented in this chapter were extracted from the British National Corpus with the help of collexeme analysis as implemented in the Treebank.info project, which makes use of dependency-parsing to improve and simplify the extraction of collexemes (cf. Proisl and Uhrig 2012, Uhrig & Proisl 2012). The rankings are based on log-likelihood.

Table 1.5 Verbs used in the ditransitive construction in ICE-GB: IT∈CX1, IT∋CX2 and collostructional strength compare (Stefanowitsch and Gries 2003)

	Ditransitive uses (Mukherjee 2005)	Total of verb tokens	IT∈CX1		IT∋CX2		Collostructional analysis (Stefanowitsch and Gries 2003)	
			Rank	Value	Rank	Value	Rank	c. strength
Give	562	1221	1	32.28%	4	46.03%	1	0
Tell	491	794	2	28.20%	3	61.84%	2	1.60E-127
Ask	91	518	3	5.23%	19	17.57%	26	6.28E-04
Show	84	659	4	4.82%	22	12.75%	5	2.23E-33
Send	79	350	5	4.54%	18	22.57%	3	7.26E-68
Offer	54	198	6	3.10%	12	27.27%	4	3.31E-49
Get	34	3646	7	1.95%	56	0.93%		
Do	27	8214	8	1.55%	66	0.33%		
Cost	23	65	9	1.32%	7	35.38%	6	1.12E-22
Teach	23	92	10	1.32%	17	25.00%	7	4.32E-16
Allow	19	331	11	1.09%	32	5.74%	9	1.12E-10
Pay	18	434	12	1.03%	39	4.15%	19	2.34E-05
Assure	13	19	13	0.75%	2	68.42%		
Lend	12	31	14	0.69%	6	38.71%	10	2.85E-09
Promise	12	43	15	0.69%	11	27.91%	13	3.23E-08
Buy	12	228	16	0.69%	35	5.26%	22	8.35E-05
Take	12	1655	17	0.69%	61	0.73%		
Wish	9	156	18	0.52%	31	5.77%	17	3.11E-06
Cause	9	244	19	0.52%	43	3.69%	25	5.56E-04
Owe	8	25	20	0.46%	8	32.00%	12	2.67E-08
Grant	8	27	21	0.46%	9	29.63%	15	1.33E-06
Deny	8	51	22	0.46%	20	15.69%	11	4.50E-09
Earn	8	56	23	0.46%	21	14.29%	14	2.13E-07
Leave	8	629	24	0.46%	51	1.27%		
Award	7	16	25	0.40%	5	43.75%	8	1.36E-11
Guarantee	7	27	26	0.40%	13	25.93%	21	4.72E-05
Bring	7	461	27	0.40%	50	1.52%		
Charge	5	44	28	0.29%	23	11.36%	24	3.02E-04
Hand	5	156	29	0.29%	44	3.21%	20	3.01E-05
Write	5	438	30	0.29%	52	1.14%		
Total number of verbs occurring in the ditransitive construction in ICE-GB: 71								

Table 1.6 Top collexemes for the NP slots of the ditransitive construction (BNC; treebank.info; log-likelihood)[a]

NP1	I, he, you, they, it, we, she, this, me, someone, god, people, goal, doctor, man, father, somebody, mother, government, company, magistrate, victory, act, friend, penalty, nobody, system, section, minister
NP2	me, him, you, us, them, her, it, yourself, himself, people, herself, half, themselves, 'em, myself, taxpayer, users, company, everyone, students, home, readers, ourselves
NP3	Chance, opportunity, money, bit, something, way, look, smile, time, each, idea, name, pounds, hour, glance, pleasure, lift, confidence, lot, anything, pound, information, ring, lead, kiss, advantage, power, advice, truth, right

[a]BNC search carried out with treebank.info: [nsubj – verb lemma – indirect obj – direct obj]; ranks based on log-likelihood; obvious parsing errors were eliminated

4.1 A Collostructional Analysis of the NP Slots of the Ditransitive Construction Does Not Make Much Sense

We have seen that a collostructional analysis of the verbs occurring in the ditransitive construction serves well to characterize the construction as such since the verbs express "transfer" to a greater or lesser degree. This does not apply in quite the same way to the collexemes of the other slots of the ditransitive construction, but, as can be seen in Table 1.6, all the top collexemes in the NP2 (active indirect object) slot refer to people (with the albeit important exception of *it*), whereas those in the NP3 (active direct object) slot refer to objects or abstract entities.

Nevertheless, such a list of collexemes does not serve particularly well as a characterization of the construction. And there is an obvious explanation: More than 50% of all uses in the ditransitive construction in the BNC are uses of *give*, and this, quite obviously, shows in the list of collexemes.

What this means is that it is much more revealing (in the case of the ditransitive, at least) to consider the collexemes of the general construction when being used with particular verbs. This takes us to a less abstract level of construction, namely, item-based constructions such as "the ditransitive construction with *give*". Since this kind of construction is a constructionist representation of the valency properties of the respective item, I refer to this level of constructions as valency constructions (Herbst and Schüller 2008, Herbst 2011a, 2014a, b).

4.2 Characterizing the Complement Slots of Valency Constructions

Irrespective of whether one takes a constructionist view of valency or not, a description of the complement slots of the construction (or the complements of a valency carrier) always involves a formal characterization (in terms of the

Table 1.7 Characterization of nominative complement (Sn) and the accusative complement (Sa) of the verb *anziehen* ("'dress'") (Helbig and Schenkel 1969: 276)

Sn ➔	Hum (*Die Frau* zieht *das Kind* an.)
Sa ➔	1. Hum (Die Mutter zieht *das Kind* an.) 2. –Anim (Kleidungsstücke) (Die Frau zieht *das Kleid* an.) 3. Sa = Sn (Refl)(Die Frau zieht *sich* an.)

Table 1.8 Description of the nominative and accusative complements of *beachten* (sense 1) in *VALBU* (2004) (my translation in brackets, TH)

NomE: derjenige, der etwas einhält: Person/Institution (someone observing something: person/institution)
AkkE: dasjenige, das eingehalten wird: Objekt [Regularität] (something that is being observed: object [regularity])

Table 1.9 Description of sense A of the verb *keep* in *A Valency Dictionary of English* (2004)

Keep can mean "remain"
(i) **Something such as food can keep**, i.e. keep fresh
(ii) **Someone or something can keep in a particular condition** (often used with adjectives such as *quiet, silent, fresh, young, dry*)
(iii) **Someone or something can keep to a path, course of action or a limit**, i.e. not leave or exceed it

phrases/clauses) and a characterization of valency slots with respect to meaning and/or the lexical items that can occur in them (described as valency stratification by Almela et al. 2011). Various models of valency theory have chosen different methods to achieve such a characterization:

Semantic Features The first valency dictionary of German—the *Wörterbuch zur Valenz und Distribution deutscher Verben* by Helbig and Schenkel (1969/^{2}1973)—employs semantic components such as + Hum or – Anim (Table 1.7).

Semantic Roles Later, Helbig (1992: 155) argues in favour of including semantic roles such as "agens, patiens, lokativ, adressat, instrumental".[6] While this method serves well to identify the complements occurring in different patterns,[7] semantic roles are of little value when it comes to giving an indication of which lexical items occur in a particular valency slot.

Lexical Paraphrases In order to achieve a more precise semantic characterization, more recent valency dictionaries provide more specific lexical paraphrases. This is the policy taken both in *VALBU* (Schumacher et al. 2004) and *A Valency Dictionary of English* (Herbst et al. 2004) (Tables 1.8 and 1.9):

[6] Agent, patient, locative, addressee and instrumental

[7] Very occasionally, semantic roles are made use of in the complement blocks of *A Valency Dictionary of English* (Herbst et al. 2004) to serve precisely this purpose.

Table 1.10 Note for *kill* in *A Valency Dictionary of English* (2004)

(i) **A person, organization, animal, poisonous substance, natural catastrophe, bomb, etc. can kill a person, animal or plant**, i.e. cause them to die
(ii) **Something can kill a plan, idea, etc.,** i. e. prevent it from succeeding

Table 1.11 Information on the complement of *persist (in)* in *The Oxford Dictionary of Current Idiomatic English* (1975)

Interrupting, behaving unpleasantly; habit, conduct, line of action

Lists of Collocates As illustrated by the example provided in Table 1.10, the description of the complement slots provided in the notes on meaning in the *Valency Dictionary of English* takes the form of a list of collocates rather than that of a generalization.

Outside valency theory, a very similar policy was taken in the *Oxford Dictionary of Current Idiomatic English* (Cowie and Mackin 1975) by (Table 1.11).

4.3 Collo-profiles Based on Collostructional Analysis

It is perfectly obvious that semantic features or abstract semantic roles do not lend themselves to descriptions in dictionaries intended for non-specialist users. Nevertheless, the fact that lexicographers (and linguists) have found it necessary to provide relatively specific lexical information to characterize complement slots of constructions could also be taken as an indication of how such information could be stored in the human brain.

If we follow this line of thinking and combine it with collostructional analysis, then the complement slots of valency constructions can be envisaged as comprising different levels of representation. All of these may be relevant in varying degrees, depending on the items in question and maybe also on individual speakers:

- A collo-profile, representing the collo-items occurring in the complement slots of a valency construction with a rough indication of frequency in terms of font size[8]
- A semantic generalization across the meanings of the collo-items
- A semantic generalization concerning the function of the slot in the construction in terms of an argument role

[8]For a similar form of representation of the frequency of elements occurring in a construction through font size, see Bybee (2013: 61).

Table 1.12 below exemplifies the form a description of the monotransitive valency construction for the English verb *perform* could take[9]: For reasons of clarity, the IT∈CX1-values are given here as well, which, however, need not be shown in a constructicon to be used by learners, for example.[10]

Collo-profiles are also a valuable instrument to compare the use of a verb in two different constructions in a kind of distinctive collexeme analysis (Gries and Stefanowitsch 2004a), as e.g. with the mono- and ditransitive uses of *earn* illustrated in Table 1.13.

Clearly, our knowledge of language must comprise facts about valency constructions and not just about argument structure constructions. When it comes to characterizing the complement slots of the construction, the level of valency constructions is more enlightening than that of argument structure constructions. A graph such as Table 1.13 is not to be interpreted to mean that all items listed in the various slots can necessarily be expected to occur in any combination; thus the subject *goal* is rather unlikely to occur with a direct object *nickname*. In electronic versions of collo-profiles, such relations could be shown by a clicking device. Interestingly, the collo-items identified for the collo-profiles correspond to the co-collocates identified in the Lexical Constellation Model by Almela, Cantos and Sanchez (Almela et al. 2013).

5 Still Further Down: From Valency Constructions to Collocations

5.1 Collexeme Shortfall

In this section, I would like to adopt a slightly different perspective by not looking at the collexemes that show high collostructional strength or a high IT∈CX1-value, but at items that take a lower rank in the collo-profile of a valency construction than one might reasonably expect, which includes the repelled collexemes in Gries and Stefanowitsch's terminology.

For instance, there is a noticeable difference in rank between *letter*, *postcard* and *Christmas card* as collexemes of monotransitive *write*—both in a log-likelihood-based collostructional and a raw-frequency-based-ITECX analysis (Table 1.14).

What is remarkable here is that *postcard* takes a higher rank with the measure that takes overall frequency in the corpus into account than with the one that does not. Looking at monotransitive uses of *postcard* in the object slot of the monotransitive construction produces the following results (Table 1.14).

[9]Apologies to all purists, who consider the terms "transitive" and "valency" to be incompatible.
[10]It is obvious that in a general reference constructicon, it might be preferable to give only rather rough indications of frequency because precise IT∈CX-values are only valid for the corpus used anyway.

Table 1.12 Description of the divalent valency construction for *perform*[a]

perform verb			carry out	
... the participants		*performed*	*the task ... coca 2015 acad*	
np		verb	np	
mostly Person			performance	
they	8.6%	perform	function	7.1%
he	6.6%		functions	5.7%
it	4.4%		task	3.7%
we	3.7%		tasks	3.1%
you	3.7%		role	2.5%
she	2.0%		duties	2.2%
i	1.8%		service	1.6%
subjects	0.8%		operation	1.4%
person	0.8%		act	1.3%
who	0.8%		them	1.3%
group	0.7%		work	1.1%
people	0.7%		duty	1.0%
team	0.6%		miracles	1.0%
unit	0.6%		ceremony	1.0%
company	0.5%		dance	1.0%
him	0.5%		it	0.9%
one	0.5%		analysis	0.9%
doctors	0.4%		operations	0.8%
men	0.4%		trick	0.8%
system	0.4%		experiments	0.8%
those	0.4%		services	0.8%
student	0.4%		feats	0.7%
computer	0.4%		actions	0.7%
child	0.4%		best	0.7%
number	0.4%		feat	0.7%
surgeons	0.3%		experiment	0.7%
surgeon	0.3%		number	0.7%
bodies	0.3%		one	0.7%
players	0.3%		miracle	0.6%
animals	0.3%		variety	0.6%
students	0.3%		action	0.6%
members	0.3%		calculations	0.5%
us	0.3%		acts	0.5%
judges	0.3%		ritual	0.5%
machines	0.3%		activity	0.5%
jesus	0.3%		music	0.5%
users	0.3%		part	0.5%
pupils	0.3%		others.	
girls	0.3%			
model	0.3%			
systems	0.3%			
society	0.3%			
party	0.3%			
children	0.3%			
man	0.3%			
others.				

[a]Based on a treebank.info search of the BNC of the following kind: "[[{"wc":"VERB", "not_outdep":["iobj","prep_(for)"],"lemma":"perform"},{"relation":"nsubj"}, {"relation":"dobj"}], [{},{},{}],[{},{},{}]]" (explicitly excluding indirect objects and *for* prepositional phrases). The order of the elements occurring in the NP slots of the construction is determined by their IT$\in$CX1-value, i.e. the proportion of all items found in this slot in the corpus under analysis

Table 1.13 Collo-profiles for *earn* in the monotransitive and ditransitive constructions[a]

she		*earned*	*a lot of money*		*this goal*		*earned*	*them*		*3 points*	
np		verb	np		np		verb	np		np	
person			what is earned		event, ability, etc.			person, institution		what is earned	
as agent			as patient		as causer			as recipient		as patient	
he	10.2%		money	8.0%	it	5.0%				place	5.6%
you	7.4%		living	5.1%	goal	2.8%				reputation	3.4%
i	6.4%		what	3.0%	he	2.3%				nickname	3.2%
they	6.2%		it	2.4%	i	2.0%				respect	2.9%
she	3.6%		reputation	2.0%	victory	1.5%				title	2.7%
it	3.0%		interest	1.9%	which	1.5%				award	2.7%
we	2.3%		$	1.8%	skills	1.3%				money	2.4%
people	1.7%		place	1.7%	this	1.3%				name	1.9%
men	1.0%		more	1.7%	that	1.3%				points	1.7%
women	1.0%		wage	1.2%	success	1.0%				draw	1.2%
those	0.9%		respect	1.2%	one	1.0%				hour	1.2%
man	0.9%		income	1.2%	they	1.0%				$	1.2%
workers	0.8%		million	1.2%	monopolist	0.8%				right	1.2%
which	0.7%		wages	0.9%	dancing	0.8%				win	1.0%
who	0.5%		right	0.9%	achievement	0.8%				fine	1.0%
players	0.4%		return	0.9%	career	0.8%				living	1.0%
banks	0.3%		profits	0.8%	act	0.8%				million	1.0%
husband	0.3%		points	0.8%	form	0.8%				man	1.0%
father	0.3%		nickname	0.7%	you	0.8%				sobriquet	0.7%
money	0.3%		lot	0.7%	deeds	0.5%				mbe	0.7%
many	0.3%		salary	0.6%	wins	0.5%				admiration	0.7%
husbands	0.3%		pounds	0.6%	performances	0.5%		him	33.3%	promotion	0.7%
person	0.3%		rate	0.6%	courage	0.5%		them	11.0%	thousand	0.7%
children	0.3%		bonus	0.6%	habit	0.5%		it	3.7%	position	0.7%
most	0.3%		praise	0.6%	jump	0.5%		himself	3.4%	interest	0.7%
well	0.3%		bread	0.5%	penalty	0.5%		her	3.4%	point	0.7%
them	0.3%		half	0.5%	contributions	0.5%		me	3.1%	cbe	0.5%
some	0.3%		%	0.5%	goals	0.5%		you	1.8%	accolade	0.5%
worker	0.2%		commission	0.5%	display	0.5%		themselves	1.3%	exemption	0.5%
girl	0.2%		less	0.5%	standards	0.5%		us	1.3%	1000	0.5%
members	0.2%		6d	0.4%	win	0.5%		city	1.0%	trophy	0.5%
others.			others.		others.			others.		others.	

[a]Based on the BNC and treebank.info-queries of the following kind: "[[{"lemma":"earn", "not_outdep":["prep_(for)"]},{"relation":"nsubj"},{"relation":"dobj"},{"relation":"iobj"}],[{},{},{},{}],[{},{},{},{}],[{},{},{},{}]]"

Table 1.14 Comparison of the items *letter* and *postcard* in the monotransitive construction with *write* in the BNC[a]

	Frequency	Collostructional analysis		ITECX analysis	
		Rank	Log-likelihood	Rank	IT∈CX1
Letter	565	2	5347.451	2	
Postcard	5	155	23.4237	255	

[a]Treebank.info: search [verb lemma write – no indirect obj – direct obj – no prepositional *to*]; ranks based on log-likelihood; obvious parsing errors were eliminated

From the point of view of the noun *postcard* ($n = 871$), we can say that it occurs in the monotransitive construction in 15.73% of all cases (IT∋CX2) and in 0.57% with the monotransitive construction with *write*. This is much lower than we can expect on the basis of a comparison with *letter* ($n = 20{,}925$ in the BNC)[11]: if one were to assume that the proportion of the overall occurrences of the nouns *letter*

[11]Strictly speaking, one would have to subtract uses of the word *letter* referring to the letters of the alphabet or multi-word units such as *the letter of the law* (about 500 instances in the BNC).

Table 1.15 Verbs occurring in the monotransitive construction with the object *postcard* in the BNC

	Frequency	Collostructional analysis		ITECX analysis	
		Rank	Log-likelihood	Rank	IT∈CX1
Send	26	1	438.729	1	18.98%
Buy	13	2	189.7635	2	9.49%
Receive	11	3	156.1301	3	8.03%
Get	11	4	88.5783	4	8.03%
Have	10	7	29.6175	5	7.30%
Write	5	5	51.5702	6	3.65%
etc.					
Total	137				

[a]Treebank.info-search: [verb lemma – no indirect obj – direct obj: Lemma postcard noun – no prepositional *too*]; obvious parsing errors were eliminated

and *postcard* in the BNC are reflected in their occurrence in the direct object slot of the monotransitive construction with *write*, then we should either get some 120 occurrences of *write/letter* (instead of 565) or 23 of *write/postcard* (instead of 5), which, quite obviously, is not the case. Part of the explanation for this collexeme shortfall can be sought in the high IT∈CX1-value for *send* in Table 1.15.

So, if we try to overcome Bybee's (2010: 97) objection against collostructional analysis—"that lexemes do not occur in corpora by pure chance"—then we must compare semantically similar cases, which, however, of course, is extremely difficult to do. An attempt was made to compare the verbs used with the nouns *letter, postcard, Christmas card* and *e-mail* in COCA. The comparison is based on the same searches for the verbs *write* and *send* for the message-producing end and for *read, get* and *receive* for the message-receiving end. The figures presented in Figs. 1.1 and 1.2 must be treated with some caution, however, since COCA does not allow for searches with optional elements. Figure 1.1 shows that *read, get* and *receive* show a similar pattern for all four nouns, whereas *write* is used more frequently than *send* with *letter*, with the opposite being the case for the other three nouns[12].

The point is that the difference in meaning between *write* and *send* becomes neutralized or irrelevant in many (though not all) situations in which they are used together with a noun denoting a written message. There is no point in writing a letter without sending it, just as there is no point in sending an e-mail if it contains no text. Since speakers seem to conceptualize *writing* and *sending* as one action, there is also no point in using two verbs unless you want to tease the two actions apart, as in:

(6) *You write a letter and we'll send it. COCA 1992 SPOK*

[12]Note that occasional uses of *mail* in the sense of *e-mail* have been ignored here.

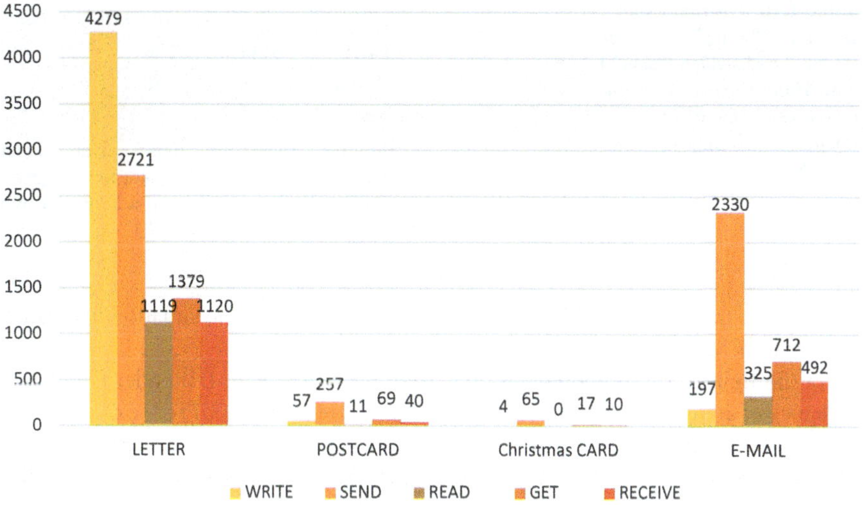

Fig. 1.1 Co-occurrence of *write*, *send*, *read*, *get*, *receive* with the nouns *letter*, *postcard*, *Christmas card* and *e-mail* in COCA

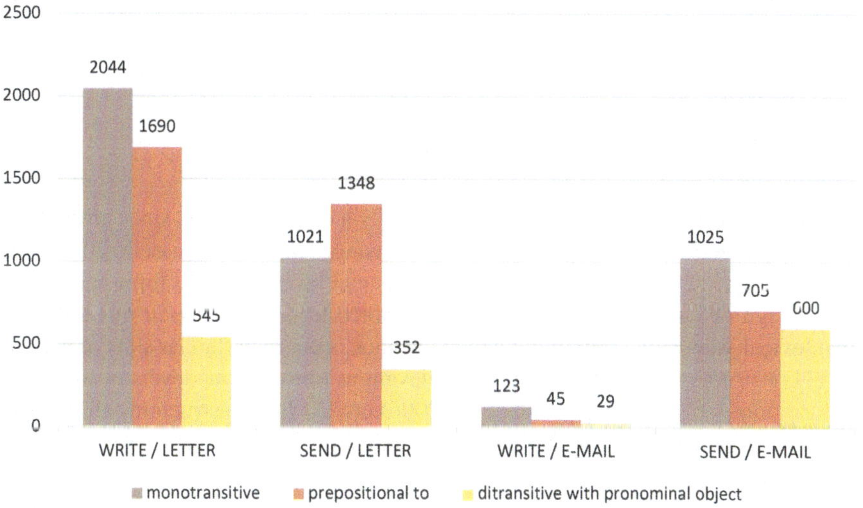

Fig. 1.2 Relation of the uses of *write* and *send* with the nouns *letter and e-mail* in the monotransitive construction, the prepositional construction with *to* and the ditransitive construction in COCA

It is easy to see that the effort involved in the writing of a letter is greater than that involved in writing a postcard, a Christmas card or an e-mail, which may be an explanation for the fact why *send* is conventionally used with these nouns in English (although the effort of sending an e-mail is also minimal). Furthermore, there is also

Table 1.16 Distribution of *schreiben* ("write"), *schicken* ("send") and *senden* ("send") with *Mail* (e-mail), *Postkarte* ("postcard") and *Brief* ("letter") according to DWDS[a]

	schreiben	schicken	senden
Brief	3144	286	55
Postkarte	88	36	7
Mail	57	61	0

[a]Figures given are those given under "Referenz- und Zeitungskorpora (aggregiert)" when one carries out a lemma search of the type "Brief schreiben"

no need for this particular bias towards *send* if we compare the situation in English with that in German (Table 1.16).

In the light of these findings, *write/letter* and *send/e-mail* fall under the classic category of collocation as defined, e.g. by Hausmann (1984, 2007) or "expressions... representing usual ways of expressing certain notions" (Langacker 2008: 19) (see also the notion of probabemes in Herbst 2011b, Klotz and Herbst 2016). Colloprofiles of different verbs can be instrumental in identifying such collocations: comparing *write* and *read* reveals further idiosyncrasies, such as that people *write* but don't *read cheques*; similarly, *read the newspaper* is quite common, but, of course, one might argue, nobody *writes a newspaper*, but then, have people who have read a newspaper really read all of it?

6 Is Language a Collostructicon?

Is language a collostructicon? Certainly not only a collostructicon, since abstraction and categorization are important aspects of language learning (Tomasello 2003) and, consequently, abstractions and categorizations can be expected to form part of our knowledge of language. However, what I wanted to demonstrate in this article is that lexical knowledge specifying which lexemes occur in particular slots of higher-level constructions is to be considered relevant at (the) various levels of linguistic description—so, to modify Goldberg's (2006) credo "It's constructions all the way down" (which should be *up* anyway), we could say "It's collexemes (or items) all the way down."

Although the insight into the essentially phraseological nature of language is by no means new—as shown by the work of Hausmann (1984) and Sinclair (2004) and many others—what is new is that constructionist approaches provide a model of language in which these phenomena are not shifted to the margin and treated as a kind of curious addendum to the real thing (Ellis 2008; Gries 2009). It has been pointed out repeatedly that the constructionist approach could and should be applied to foreign language teaching to a far greater extent than is the case at the moment (Herbst 2016a, 2017; Siepmann 2007). Most importantly, however, a collostructicon could be a central part of (learners') constructicon, which is to be envisaged as the linguistic reference work of the future overcoming traditional grammar books and dictionaries by providing information on all aspects of language on the basis of a unified theory of language (Herbst 2016b).[13] The representations of collo-profiles sketched out in Tables 1.12 and 1.13 can be imagined as part of the description of argument structure and valency constructions in such a constructicon.

References

Almela, M., Cantos, P., & Sánchez, A. (2011). Towards a dynamic combinatorial dictionary: A proposal for introducing interactions between collocations in an electronic dictionary of English word combinations. In I. Kosem & K. Kosem (Eds.), *Electronic lexicography in the 21st century: New applications for new users. Proceedings of eLex 2011, bled, 10–12 November 2011* (p. 111). Ljubljana: Trojina.

Almela, M., Cantos, P., & Sánchez, A. (2013). Collocation, co-collocation, constellation... Any advances in distributional semantics? *Procedia – Social and Behavioral Sciences, 95*, 231–240.

Bartsch, S. (2004). *Structural and functional properties of collocations in English: A corpus study of lexical and pragmatic constraints on lexical co-occurrence*. Tübingen: Narr.

Beckner, C., Blythe, R., Bybee, J., Christiansen, M. H., Croft, W., Ellis, N. C., Holland, J., Ke, J., Larsen-Freeman, D., & Schoenemann, T. [The Five Graces Group]. (2009). Language is a complex adaptive system: Position paper. *Language Learning, 59 Suppl., 1*, 1–26.

Behrens, H. (2007). The acquisition of argument structure. In T. Herbst & K. Götz-Votteler (Eds.), *Valency. Theoretical, descriptive and cognitive issues* (pp. 193–214). Berlin/New York: Mouton de Gruyter.

Behrens, H. (2009). Usage-based and emergentist approaches to language acquisition. *Linguistics, 47*(2), 383–411.

Boas, H. C. (2003). *A constructional approach to resultatives*. Stanford: CSLI Publications.

Boas, H. C. (2011). Zum Abstraktionsgrad von Resultativkonstruktionen. In S. Engelberg, A. Holler, & K. Proost (Eds.), *Sprachliches Wissen zwischen Lexikon und Grammatik* (pp. 37–69). Berlin/New York: Mouton de Gruyter.

Bybee, J. (2010). *Language, usage and cognition*. Cambridge: Cambridge University Press.

Bybee, J. (2013). Usage-based theory and exemplar representation of constructions. In T. Hoffmann & G. Trousdale (Eds.), *The Oxford handbook of construction grammar* (pp. 49–69). Oxford: Oxford University Press.

Bybee, J. (2015). *Language change*. Cambridge: Cambridge University Press.

Cowie, A. P., & Mackin, R. (1975). *Oxford dictionary of current idiomatic English. Volume 1: Verbs with prepositions & particles*. London: Oxford University Press.

Dąbrowska, E. (2015). What exactly is universal grammar, and has anyone seen it? *Frontiers in Psychology, 6*, ISSN 1664–ISSN 1078.

Dąbrowska, E., & Lieven, E. (2005). Towards a lexically specific grammar of children's question constructions. *Cognitive Linguistics, 16*(3), 437–474.

Divjak, D., & Caldwell-Harris, C. L. (2015). Frequency and entrenchment. In E. Dąbrowska, & D. Divjak (Eds.), *Handbook of cognitive linguistics*, 53–75. Berlin/Boston: De Gruyter Mouton.

Ellis, N. (2003). Constructions, chunking & connectionism: The emergence of second language structure. In C. J. Doughty & M. H. Long (Eds.), *The handbook of second language acquisition* (pp. 63–103). Malden/Oxford/Carlton: Blackwell.

[13]For related projects see Almela, Cantos & Sánchez (2011), Lyngfelt et al. (2012) or Sköldberg et al. (2013).

Ellis, N. (2008). Phraseology: The periphery and the heart of language. In F. Meunier & S. Granger (Eds.), *Phraseology in foreign language learning and teaching* (pp. 1–13). Amsterdam/Philadelphia: Benjamins.

Engelberg, S., König, S., Proost, K., & Winkler, E. (2011). Argumentstrukturmuster als Konstruktionen? Identität – Verwandtschaft – Idiosynkrasien. Engelberg, S., Holler, A., & Proost, K. (Eds.), *Sprachliches Wissen zwischen Lexikon und Grammatik* (71–112). Berlin/Boston: de Gruyter.

Evert, S. (2005). *The Statistics of word cooccurrences: Word pairs and collocations. Dissertation,* Institut für maschinelle Sprachverarbeitung, University of Stuttgart, URN urn:nbn:de:bsz:93-opus-23714.

Evert, S. (2008). Corpora and collocations. In A. Lüdeling & M. Kytö (Eds.), *Corpus linguistics. An international handbook* (pp. 1212–1248). Berlin: Mouton de Gruyter.

Faulhaber, S. (2011). *Verb valency patterns: A challenge for semantics-based accounts.* Berlin/New York: de Gruyter Mouton.

Francis, G., Hunston, S., & Manning, E. (1996). *Collins Cobuild grammar patterns. 1: Verbs.* London: HarperCollins.

Francis, G., Hunston, S., & Manning, E. (1998). *Collins Cobuild grammar patterns. 2: Nouns and adjectives.* London: HarperCollins.

Gimson, A. C. (1989). *An Introduction to the Pronunciation of English. London: Arnold: recte*

Goldberg, A. E. (1995). *Constructions: A construction grammar approach to argument structure.* Chicago: Chicago University Press.

Goldberg, A. E. (2006). *Constructions at work.* Oxford/New York: Oxford University Press.

Goldberg, A. E. (forthcoming). *Explain me this.* Princeton: Princeton University Press.

Goldberg, A. E., & Herbst, T. (in prep). The nice of you construction: A usage-based constructionist analysis.

Gries, S. T. (2009). Phraseology and linguistic theory: A brief survey. In S. Granger & F. Meunier (Eds.), *Phraseology. An interdisciplinary perspective* (pp. 3–25). Amsterdam/Philadelphia: Benjamins.

Gries, S. T. (2015). More (old and new) misunderstandings of collostructional analysis: On Schmid and Küchenhoff (2013). *Cognitive Linguistics, 26*(3), 505–536.

Gries, S. T., Hampe, B., & Schönefeld, D. (2010). Converging evidence II: More on the association of verbs and constructions. In S. Rice & J. Newman (Eds.), *Empirical and experimental methods in cognitive/functional research* (pp. 59–90). Stanford: CSLI Publications.

Gries, S., & Stefanowitsch, A. (2004a). Extending collostructional analysis: A corpus-based perspective on 'alternations'. *International Journal of Corpus Linguistics, 9*(1), 97–129.

Gries, S., & Stefanowitsch, A. (2004b). Covarying collexemes in the into-causative. In M. Archard & S. Kemmer (Eds.), *Language, culture, and mind* (pp. 225–236). Stanford: CSLI.

Hampe, B., & Schönefeld, D. (2006). Syntactic Leaps or Lexical Variation? More on 'Creative Syntax. In S. Gries & A. Stefanowitsch (Eds.), *Corpora in Cognitive Linguistics: The Syntax-Lexis Interface* (pp. 127–157). Berlin, New York: Mouton de Gruyter.

Hausmann, F.-J. (1984). Wortschatzlernen ist Kollokationslernen. *Praxis des neusprachlichen Unterrichts, 31*, 395–406.

Hausmann, F.-J. (2007). Die Kollokationen im Rahmen der Phraseologie: Systematische und historische Darstellung. *Zeitschrift für Anglistik und Amerikanistik, 55*(3), 217–235.

Helbig, G. (1992). *Probleme der Valenz- und Kasustheorie.* Tübingen: Niemeyer.

Helbig, G., & Schenkel, W. (1969/[2]1973). *Wörterbuch zur Valenz und Distribution deutscher Verben.* Leipzig: Verlag Enzyklopädie.

Herbst, T. (2009). Valency: Item-specificity and idiom principle. In U. Römer & R. Schulze (Eds.), *Exploring the Lexis-Grammar Interface* (pp. 49–68). Amsterdam: John Benjamins.

Herbst, Thomas. 2010. Valency constructions and clause constructions or how, if at all, valency grammarians might sneeze the foam off the cappuccino In Hans JöSchmid & Susanne Handl *Cognitive Foundations of Linguistic Usage Patterns: Empirical Studies*, 225–255. Berlin/New York: de Gruyter Mouton.

Herbst, T. (2011a). The status of generalizations: Valency and argument structure constructions. *Zeitschrift für Anglistik und Amerikanistik, 59*(4), 347–367.

Herbst, T. (2011b). Choosing sandy beaches – Collocations, probabemes and the idiom principle. In T. Herbst, S. Faulhaber, & P. Uhrig (Eds.), *A phraseological view of language: A tribute to John Sinclair* (pp. 27–57). Berlin/New York: de Gruyter Mouton.

Herbst, T. (2014a). The valency approach to argument structure constructions. In T. Herbst, H.-J. Schmid, & S. Faulhaber (Eds.), *Constructions – Collocations – Patterns* (pp. 167–216). Berlin/Boston: de Gruyter Mouton.

Herbst, T. (2014b). Idiosyncrasies and generalizations: Argument structure, semantic roles and the valency realization principle. In M. Hilpert & S. Flach (Eds.), *Yearbook of the German cognitive linguistics association, Jahrbuch der Deutschen Gesellschaft für Kognitive Linguistik, Vol. II* (pp. 253–289). Berlin/München/Boston: de Gruyter Mouton.

Herbst, T. (2016a). Foreign language learning is construction learning – What else? Moving towards pedagogical construction grammar. In S. de Knop, & G. Gilquin (Eds.), *Applied Construction Grammar*, (pp. 21–51). Berlin/Boston: de Gruyter Mouton.

Herbst, T. (2016b). Wörterbuch war gestern. Programm für ein unifiziertes Konstruktikon! In S. J. Schierholz, R. H. Gouws, Z. Hollós, & W. Wolski (Eds.), *Wörterbuchforschung und Lexikographie*. Berlin/Boston: de Gruyter.

Herbst, T. (2017). Grünes Licht für pädagogische Konstruktionsgrammatik – Denn: Linguistik ist nicht (mehr) nur Chomsky. *Fremdsprachen Lehren und Lernen, 46*, 119–135.

Herbst, T., Heath, D., Roe, I. F., & Götz, D. (2004). *A valency dictionary of English*. London/New York: Mouton de Gruyter.

Herbst, T., & Schüller, S. [now Faulhaber]. (2008). Introduction to syntactic analysis. *A Valency approach*. Tübingen: Narr.

Hoffmann, T., & Trousdale, G. (2013). Construction grammar: Introduction. In T. Hoffmann & G. Trousdale (Eds.), *The Oxford handbook of construction grammar* (pp. 1–12). Oxford: Oxford University Press.

Jacobs, J. (2009). Valenzbindung oder Konstruktionsbindung? Eine Grundfrage der Grammatiktheorie. *ZGL, 37*, 490–513.

Klotz, M., & Herbst, T. (2016). *English dictionaries. A linguistic introduction*. Berlin: Schmidt.

Langacker, R. W. (1987). *Foundations of cognitive grammar. volume I: Theoretical prerequisites*. Stanford: Stanford University Press.

Langacker, R. W. (2008). *Cognitive grammar. a basic introduction*. Oxford: Oxford University Press.

Lieven, E. (2014). First language learning from a usage-based approach. In T. Herbst, H. J. Schmid, & S. Faulhaber (Eds.), *Constructions, collocations, patterns* (pp. 9–32). Berlin/Boston: De Gruyter Mouton.

Lyngfelt, B., Borin, L., Forsberg, M., Prentice, J., Rydstedt, R., Sköldberg, E., & Tingsell, S. (2012). Adding a constructicon to the Swedish resource network of Språkbanken. In J. Jancsary (Ed.), *Proceedings of KONVENS 2012* (pp. 452–461). http://www.oegai.at/konvens2012/proceedings/66_lyngfelt12w/.

Mukherjee, J. (2005). *English Ditransitive verbs. Aspects of theory, description and a usage-based model*. Amsterdam/New York: Rodopi.

Pecina, P. (2010). Lexical association measures and collocation extraction. *Language resources and evaluation, 44*(1), 137–158.

Perek, F. (2015). *Argument structure in usage-based construction grammar*. Amsterdam/Philadelphia: Benjamins.

Proisl, T. (in preparation). The cooccurrence of linguistic structures. [working title] Erlangen: PhD thesis.

Proisl, T., & Uhrig, P. (2012). Efficient dependency graph matching with the IMS open corpus workbench. In N. Calzolari, K. Choukri, T. Declerck, M. U. Doğan, B. Maegaard, J. Mariani, J. Odijk, & S. Piperidis (Eds.), *Proceedings of the eighth international conference on language resources and evaluation (LREC '12)* (pp. 2750–2756). Istanbul: European Language Resources Association (ELRA).

Schmid, H.-J. (2000). *English abstract nouns as conceptual shells. From Corpus to cognition.* Berlin/New York: Mouton de Gruyter.

Schmid, H. J., & Küchenhoff, H. (2013). Collostructional analysis and other ways of measuring lexicogrammatical attraction: Theoretical premises, practical problems and cognitive underpinnings. *Cognitive Linguistics, 24*(3), 531–577.

Schumacher, H., Kubczak, J., Schmidt, R., & de Ruiter, V. (2004). *VALBU – Valenzwörterbuch deutscher Verben*. Tübingen: Narr.

Siepmann, D. (2007). Wortschatz und Grammatik: zusammenbringen, was zusammengehört. *Beiträge zur Fremdsprachenvermittlung, 46*, 59–80.

Sinclair, J. (1991). *Corpus, concordance, collocation*. Oxford: Oxford University Press.

Sinclair, J. (2004). *Trust the text*. London/New York: Routledge.

Sköldberg, E., Bäckström, L., Borin, L., Forsberg, M., Lyngfelt, B., Olsson, L.-J., Prentice, J., Rydstedt, R., Tingsell, S., & Uppström, J. (2013). Between grammars and dictionaries: A Swedish constructicon. In *Proceedings of eLex 2013* (pp. 310–327).

Stefanowitsch, A., & Gries, S. T. (2003). Collostructions: Investigating the interaction of words and constructions. *International Journal of Corpus Linguistics, 8*(2), 209–243.

Stefanowitsch, A. (2011a). Keine Grammatik ohne Konstruktionen: Ein logisch-ökonmisches Argument für die Konstruktionsgrammatik. In S. Engelberg, A. Holler, & K. Proost (Eds.), *Sprachliches Wissen zwischen Lexikon und Grammatik* (pp. 181–210). Berlin/Boston: de Gruyter.

Stefanowitsch, A. (2011b). Argument structure: Item-based or distributed? *Zeitschrift für. Anglistik und Amerikanistik, 59*(4), 369–386.

Stefanowitsch, A. (2014). Collostructional analysis. A case study of the English into-causative. In T. Herbst, H.-J. Schmid, & S. Faulhaber (Eds.), *Constructions – Collocations – Patterns* (pp. 217–238). Berlin/Boston: De Gruyter Mouton.

Tomasello, M. (2003). *Constructing a language*. Cambridge, MA/London: Harvard University Press.

Uhrig, P., & Proisl, T. (2012). Less hay, more needles - using dependency-annotated corpora to provide lexicographrs with more accurate lists of collocation candidates. *Lexicographica, 28*, 141–180. https://doi.org/10.1515/lexi.2012-0009.

Welke, K. (2011). *Valenzgrammatik des Deutschen: Eine Einführung*. Berlin/New York: de Gruyter.

BNC. *The British National Corpus*. Distributed by Oxford University Computing Services on behalf of the BNC Consortium. http://www.natcorp.ox.ac.uk/.

COCA = Davies, Mark. (2008). *The Corpus of Contemporary American English: 520 million words, 1990-present*. Available online at http://corpus.byu.edu/coca/.

DWDS = Berlin-Brandenburgische Akademie der Wissenschaften. *Digitales Wörterbuch der deutschen Sprache.*https://www.dwds.de. [accessed August 2017].

Chapter 2
Bridging Collocational and Syntactic Analysis

Violeta Seretan

Abstract The advent of the computer era, which enabled the development of large text corpora and of sophisticated corpus processing tools, led to unprecedented advances in the area of collocational analysis. These advances were paralleled by significant achievements in the area of syntactic analysis, with parsing technologies becoming available for an increasing number of languages. But more often than not, these developments have taken place independently. The coupling of collocational and syntactic analyses has seldom been considered, despite the fact that one type of analysis could benefit the other. In this chapter, we focus on the integration of syntactic parsing and collocational analysis. First, we review the literature describing syntactically-informed approaches to collocation extraction. Second, we survey the work devoted to exploiting collocational resources for syntactic parsing. Finally, we refer to more recent work that proposes a joint approach to collocational and syntactic analysis, arguing that the two analyses are interdependent to such a degree that only a simultaneous process, one in which structure decoding and pattern identification go hand in hand, can provide a solid bridge between them.

1 Introduction

Quantitative methods have flourished in language-related fields of the humanities, such as linguistics, language learning, or lexicography, ever since the advent of the computer era, which enabled the development of electronic text corpora and of corpus processing technology (Nugues, 2014). These disciplines witnessed the emergence of new subfields, such as corpus linguistics, computational linguistics, computational lexicography and computer-assisted language learning, in which

---

V. Seretan (✉)
University of Geneva, Geneva, Switzerland

University of Lausanne, Lausanne, Switzerland
e-mail: violeta.seretan@unige.ch

P. Cantos-Gómez, M. Almela-Sánchez (eds.), *Lexical Collocation Analysis*, Quantitative Methods in the Humanities and Social Sciences,
https://doi.org/10.1007/978-3-319-92582-0_2

collocational analysis – that is, the analysis of patterns of words through techniques like association measures and concordancing – plays an essential role in the study of language. Collocational expressions – e.g. *bright idea*, *heavy smoker*, *break record*, *meet needs* and *deeply sorry* – represent 'the way words combine in a language to produce natural-sounding speech and writing' (Lea and Runcie, 2002, vii); therefore, collocational knowledge has far-reaching implications.

Before computerised tools for corpus processing became available, collocational analysis work has been done manually in different contexts. For instance, in a linguistic context, Maurice Gross compiled very comprehensive information on French nouns, verbs and adverbs (Gross, 1984). In a second language learning context, Harold Palmer and his successor Albert Sydney Hornby carried out pioneering work on compiling lists of frequent collocations. Their work led to the future series of collocation dictionaries known today as the *Oxford Advanced Learner's Dictionary*, one of the major references for the English language (Hornby et al., 1948).

Collocations are important not only for linguistics and lexicographic descriptions, but also for natural language processing and human-computer interaction. As stated by Sag et al. (2002, 2), collocations, along with other types of multi-word expressions or 'idiosyncratic interpretations that cross word boundaries', are 'a pain in the neck for NLP [natural language processing]'. Multi-word expressions are an area of active research in the NLP community, as attested by sustained initiatives, for instances, special interest groups and associations, international projects, book series and scientific events (for an up-to-date review, see Monti et al. 2018). But what makes collocations particularly important is their prevalence in language: 'L'importance des collocations réside dans leur omniprésence' (Mel'čuk, 2003, 26).

The computer-based collocation identification in corpora, known as collocation extraction, has a long tradition. Over the recent decades, a significant body of work has been devoted to the computational analysis of text with the purpose of compiling collocational resources for computerised lexicography, computer-assisted language learning and natural language processing, among others. One of the first large-scale research projects in this area was COBUILD, the Collins Birmingham University International Language Database (Sinclair, 1995). To date, collocation extraction work has been carried out not only for English but for many other languages, including, but not limited to, German, French, Italian, and Korean (as shown in Sects. 2 and 3). Outside an academic setting, commercial software tools such as Sketch Engine (Kilgarriff et al., 2004) and Antidote (Charest et al., 2007) became available that perform collocation extraction from corpora for lexicographic purposes.

In general, the focus of automatic collocation extraction work was on developing appropriate statistical methods, able to pinpoint good collocation candidates in the immense dataset of possible word combinations that quantitative methods consider as their input – a task which has traditionally been described by using the metaphor 'looking for needles in a haystack' (Choueka, 1988). However, purely statistical methods reach their limits as far as low-frequency candidates are concerned. They tend to ignore patterns occurring less than a handful of times, and by doing so they exclude most of the candidates. Consequently, as Piao et al. (2005, 379) explain, 'the usefulness of pure statistical approaches in practical NLP applications is limited'. It soon became obvious that collocation extraction must have recourse to linguistic information in order to 'obtain an optimal result' (Piao et al., 2005, 379).

Syntax-based approaches to collocation extraction put emphasis on the accurate selection of the candidate dataset in the first place. Returning to the 'needles in a haystack' metaphor, syntax-based collocation extraction focuses on optimising the haystack and transforming it into a much smaller pile, containing less hay and more needles.[1] When collocation analysis methods are coupled to syntactic analysis methods, the input dataset is built in a more careful way, which considers the syntactic relationship between the candidate words, rather than blindly associating any co-occurring words.

In this chapter, we review existing work that combines collocational and syntactic analysis and discuss current trends on coupling these two tasks into a synchronous process, one in which structure decoding and collocation identification go hand in hand to offer an efficient solution benefiting both tasks.

2 Using Syntactic Information for Collocation Identification

Generally speaking, the architecture of a collocation extraction system can be described as a sequence of two main processing modules, preceded by an optional preprocessing module.

Linguistic preprocessing The input corpora are first split into sentences; then, for each sentence, linguistically motivated filters are applied in order to discard the items that are considered uninteresting (e.g. conjunctions and determiners). In addition, this module performs text normalisation. During this stage, a lemmatiser is typically used in order to reduce inflected word forms like *goes*, *went* and *going* to base word forms (*go*).

Stage 1: Candidate selection Based on the preprocessed version of the input, a selection procedure takes place in order to build a collocation candidate list. This procedure uses specific filters in order to decide which combinations of co-occurring words will be considered for inclusion in the candidate list. Traditionally, the filters allow for any word combination to be considered as a collocation candidate, as long as there are no more than four intervening words (hence the name 'window method'). When part-of-speech information is available, the filters request that candidate combinations match one of the patterns in a list of allowed collocation patterns (e.g. noun-noun, noun-preposition-noun, noun-verb, verb-adverb, etc.).[2]

[1]The same metaphor is used by Uhrig and Proisl (2012).

[2]Although there is no generally accepted list of collocation patterns (as it is widely accepted that the parameters of a collocation extraction procedure may vary according to the intended use of results),

Stage 2: Candidate ranking Given the list of collocation candidates from Step 1, a statistical procedure is applied in order to rank candidates according to their likelihood to constitute collocations. The simplest ranking procedure is raw frequency, which lists candidates from the most frequent to the least frequent ones. Often, in order to reduce the candidate dataset to a manageable size, a frequency threshold is applied, which discards all candidates that occur less than a given number of times (e.g. five or ten times).[3]

It is worth noting that no extraction system is devoid of error. The output is to be interpreted by professional lexicographers in order to decide on the relevance of a particular candidate or corpus-based usage sample identified. Caution should also be applied to the parameters of the extraction system: No one-size-fits-all solution exists, and the choices pertaining to corpus size, preprocessing method, window size, filters, ranking method, frequency threshold, etc. must be weighted by taking into account the intended purpose of the results (Evert and Krenn, 2005).

2.1 *Statistical Processing*

As stated in Sect. 1, the focus of most work devoted to collocation extraction has been on advancing the state of the art of the candidate ranking stage, that is, finding ways to pinpoint good collocation candidates in the immense dataset of initial candidates. (As we will discuss later in Sect. 2.2, considerably less attention has been devoted to the preceding stage, namely, that of candidate selection.)

Over the years – and particularly since the adoption of the mutual information measure from the information theory field as a way to model lexical association (Church and Hanks, 1990) – most research efforts have been spent on the statistics of lexical association. Some of the most representative works include Daille (1994), Evert (2004) and Pecina (2008).

In a nutshell, any method aimed at ranking collocation candidates (also called a lexical association measure) is a formula that computes a score for a collocation candidate, given the following information:

- the number of times the first word appears in the candidate dataset (as the first item of a candidate),

most authors agree that typical collocation patterns include the ones enumerated in Hausmann's definition (1989, 1010) – 'We shall call collocation a characteristic combination of two words in a structure like the following: (a) noun + adjective (epithet); (b) noun + verb; (c) verb + noun (object); (d) verb + adverb; (e) adjective + adverb; (f) noun + (prep) + noun'.

[3]This decision is also motivated by statistical considerations, as most statistical methods are unreliable for low-frequency data. However, it is contested by the lexicographic community, because a significant part of lexicographically interesting candidates occurs only once or twice in a corpus (Piao et al., 2005, 379).

Table 2.1 Candidate ranking: contingency table

	Word 2	Any word different from word 2
Word 1	*a*	*b*
Any word different from word 1	*c*	*d*

- the number of times the second word appears in the candidate dataset (as the second item of a candidate),
- the number of times the two words appear together (as the first and second item, respectively), and
- the total size of the candidate dataset.

A so-called contingency table is used to synthesise this information (cf. Table 2.1). The letters a, b, c and d represent the frequency 'signature' of the collocation candidate being scored (Evert, 2004).

The correspondence between the letters and the above-stated quantities is established as follows:

- the number of times the first word appears in the candidate dataset (as the first item of a candidate): $a + b$
- the number of times the second word appears in the candidate dataset (as the second item of a candidate): $a + c$
- the number of times the two words appear together (as the first and second item, respectively): a
- the total size of the candidate dataset: $a + b + c + d$.

While the quantities a, b, and c can be computed straightforwardly given the candidate dataset, the number d is to be computed by subtracting the values a, b and c from the total dataset size (usually denoted by N):

$$d = N - (a + b + c) \tag{2.1}$$

Equivalently, since it is easier to compute the quantities $a + b$, $a + c$ (which are called marginal frequencies) and a (which is called joint frequency), we can compute d as follows:

$$d = N - (a + b) - (a + c) + a. \tag{2.2}$$

For the sake of example, we provide below the explicit formula of the log-likelihood ratio association measure, which is one of the most widely used measures for collocation extraction (Dunning, 1993).

$$
\begin{aligned}
LLR = 2(&a\log a + b\log b + c\log c + d\log d - \\
&(a+b)\log(a+b) - (a+c)\log(a+c) - \\
&(b+d)\log(b+d) - (c+d)\log(c+d) + \\
&(a+b+c+d)\log(a+b+c+d))
\end{aligned}
\tag{2.3}
$$

An implementation of the computation described above is available, for pedagogical purposes, in the FipsCo Collocation Extraction Toy available in the GitHub software repository.[4] For a comprehensive list of lexical association measures, the interested reader is referred to Pecina (2005, 2008).

From discussing collocation candidate ranking methods, we will now turn to discussing the quality of the information taken into account by such methods.

2.2 *Linguistic Preprocessing and Candidate Selection*

The quality of a collocation extraction system is conditioned by the quality of the candidate dataset. No statistical processing, whatever performant, can improve the quality of the candidate collocational expressions. Given that the extraction output is nothing else than a permutation of the initial candidate list, the importance of linguistic preprocessing and candidate selection becomes evident.

Over the years, there have been repeated calls from researchers working on collocation extraction to use syntactic parsing for collocation extraction. Despite the focus on statistical methods for candidate ranking, there were several early reports acknowledging the fact that successful collocation extraction, particularly for languages other than English, is only possible when performing a careful selection of candidates by using linguistic, as opposed to linear proximity criteria. In the remaining of this section, we review some of the work that stressed the importance of syntax-based collocation extraction.

One of the earliest and better-documented reports in this area is Lafon (1984). The author extracted significant co-occurrences of words from plain French text by considering (oriented, then non-oriented) pairs in a collocational span and by using the *z-score* as an association measure. The preprocessing step consisted in detecting sentence boundaries and ruling out functional words (i.e. non-content words, where a content word is a main verb, a noun, an adjective or an adverb). The author noted that verbs rarely occur among the results, probably as a consequence of the high dispersion among different forms (Lafon, 1984, 193). Indeed, French is a language with a rich morphology,[5] and, in the absence of lemmatisation, the frequency 'signature' values are shrunk, leading to low collocation scores. Apart

[4] https://github.com/seretan/collocation-extraction-toy (accessed 1 February 2018).

[5] A French verb, for instance, may have as many as 48 forms (Tzoukermann and Radev, 1996).

from the lack of lemmatisation, the author also identified the lack of syntactic analysis as one of the main sources of problems faced during extraction. The author pointed out that any interpretation of results should be preceded by the examination of results through concordancing (Lafon, 1984, 201).

A similar report is provided by Breidt (1993) for German. Because syntactic tools for German were not available at that time, Breidt (1993) simulated parsing and used a five-word collocation span to extract verb-noun pairs (such as *[in] Betracht kommen*, 'to be considered', *or [zur] Ruhe kommen*, 'get some peace'). The author used mutual information (MI) and *t-score* as lexical association measures and compared the extraction performance in a variety of settings: different corpus and window size, presence/absence of lemmatisation, part-of-speech (POS) tagging and (simulated) parsing. The author argued that extraction from German text is more difficult than from English text, because of the much richer inflexion for verbs, the variable word order and the positional ambiguity of arguments. She explained that even distinguishing subjects from objects is very difficult in German without parsing. The result analysis showed that in order to exclude unrelated nouns, a smaller window of size 3 is preferable. However, this solution comes at the expense of recall, as valid candidates in long distance dependencies are missed. Parsing (which was simulated by eliminating the pairs in which the noun is not the object of the co-occurring verb) was shown to lead to a much higher precision of the extraction results. In addition, it was found that lemmatisation alone does not help, because it promotes new spurious candidates. The study concluded that a good level of precision can only be achieved in German with parsing: 'Very high precision rates, which are an indispensable requirement for lexical acquisition, can only realistically be envisaged for German with parsed corpora' (Breidt, 1993, 82).

For the English language, one of the earliest and most popular collocation extraction systems was Xtract (Smadja, 1993). The author relied on heuristics such as the systematic occurrence of two words at the same distance in text, in order to detect 'rigid' noun phrases (e.g. *stock market*, *foreign exchange*), phrasal templates (e.g. *common stocks rose *NUMBER* to *NUMBER**) and flexible combinations involving a verb, which the author calls predicative collocations (e.g. *index [. . .] rose*, *stock [. . .] jumped*, *use [. . .] widely*). Syntactic parsing is used in the extraction pipeline in a postprocessing, rather than preprocessing, stage, and ungrammatical results were ruled out. Evaluation by a professional lexicographer showed that parsing led to a substantial increase in the extraction performance, from 40% to 80%. The author noted that 'Ideally, in order to identify lexical relations in a corpus one would need to first parse it to verify that the words are used in a single phrase structure' (Smadja, 1993, 151).

One of the first hybrid approaches to collocation extraction, combining linguistic and statistical information, was Daille's (1994). The author relied on lemmatisation, part-of-speech tagging and shallow parsing in order to extract French compound noun terms defined by specific patterns, such as noun-adjective, noun-noun, noun-*à*-noun, noun-*de*-noun and noun-preposition-determiner-noun (e.g. *réseau national à satellites*, 'national satellite network'). Daille's shallow parsing approach consisted in applying finite state automata over sequences of POS tags. For candidate ranking, the author implemented a high number of association measures, including MI and LLR. The performance of these measures was tested against a domain-specific terminology dictionary and against a gold standard set which was manually created from the source corpus with help from experts. One of the most important findings of the study was that a high number of terms have a low frequency ($a \leq 2$). LLR was selected as a preferred measure because it was found to perform well on all corpus sizes and to promote less frequent candidates (Daille, 1994, 173). The author argued that by relying on finite state automata for linguistically preprocessing the corpora, it became possible to extract candidates from very heterogeneous environments, without having to impose a limit on the distance between composing words. This shallow parsing method led to a substantial increase in performance over the window method. According to the author, linguistic knowledge helps to drastically improve the quality of statistical systems (Daille, 1994, 192).

After syntactic parsers became available for German, researchers provided additional insights on the need of syntactic information for successful collocation extraction in this language. For instance, Krenn (2000) extracted P-N-V collocations in German (e.g. *zur Verfügung stellen*, lit., *at the availability put*, 'make available'; *am Herzen liegen*, lit., *at the heart lie*, 'have at hearth'). The author relied on POS tagging and partial parsing, i.e. syntactic constituent detection. She compared various association measures, including MI and LLR. Since syntactic information, the set of candidates identified is argued to contain less noise than if retrieved without such information. The author regrets that the window method is still largely used, 'even though the advantage of employing more detailed linguistic information for collocation identification is nowadays largely agreed upon' (Krenn, 2000, 210). On the same lines, Evert (2004), who carried out substantial joint work with Krenn, explained that 'ideally, a full syntactic analysis of the source corpus would allow us to extract the cooccurrence directly from parse trees' (Evert, 2004, 31).

A similar comment is made by Pearce (2002, 1530), who did experimental work for English and argued that 'with recent significant increases in parsing efficiency and accuracy, there is no reason why explicit parse information should not be used'. In a previous study, Pearce (2001) extracted collocations from English treebanks, i.e. corpora manually annotated with syntactic information.[6]

Additional reports on the necessity of performing a syntactic analysis as a preprocessing step in collocation extraction came from authors that attempted to apply methods originally devised for English to new languages, exhibiting richer morphology and freer word order. For instance, Shimohata et al. (1997) attempted to apply to Korean corpora the extraction techniques proposed for English by Smadja (1993). The authors stated that such techniques are unapplicable to Korean because of the freer word order. Villada Moirón (2005) attempted to identify preposition-noun-verb candidates in Dutch by relying on partial parsing (constituent detection). She showed that partial parsing is impractical for Dutch, because of the syntactic flexibility and free word order of this language. In the same vein, Huang et al.

[6]The same approach has been used by Uhrig and Proisl (2012), among others.

(2005) intended to use POS information and regular expression patterns borrowed from the Sketch Engine (Kilgarriff et al., 2004) to extract collocations from Chinese corpora. The authors pointed out that an adaptation of these patterns for Chinese was necessary in order to cope with syntactic differences and the richer POS tagset.

3 Syntax-Based Extractors

As shown in the previous section, in early collocation extraction work, integrating syntactic parsing in the extraction pipeline was often seen as an ideal, because robust and fast parsers were unavailable for most languages. The past two decades, however, have witnessed rapid advances in the parsing field, thanks, in particular, to the development of statistical dependency parsers for an increasing number of languages (Nivre, 2006; Rani et al., 2015). But despite these advances, a large body of works in the area of collocation extraction still remained linguistically agnostic. Below we review some of the most notable exceptions, which exploited syntactic parsing for improving the performance of collocation extraction.

One of the most important exceptions is Lin (1998, 1999), which describes a syntax-based collocation extraction approach for English based on dependency parsing. Collocation candidates are identified as word pairs linked by a head-dependent relation. The advantage of this approach is that there is no a priori limitation for the distance between two items in a candidate pair, as in the traditional window-based approach. Since the dependency parser is prone to errors, especially for the longer sentences, the author decided to exclude from the input corpus the sentences longer than 25 words. In addition, the author had attempted to semiautomatically correct some parsing errors before proceeding to the identification of collocation candidates based on the parser output. Evaluation was carried out on a small portion of the top-scored results and showed that 9.7% of the candidates were still affected by parsing errors (Lin, 1999, 320).

A similar work was performed for English and Chinese by Wu, Lü and Zhou (Wu and Zhou, 2003; Lü and Zhou, 2004). In their systems, collocation candidates are identified from syntactically analysed text. A parser is used to identify pairs of words linked by syntactic relations of type verb-object, noun-adjective and verb-adverb. Evaluation was performed on a sample of 2000 pairs that were randomly selected among the top-scored results according the LLR score. The results showed a similar rate of error due to parsing, namely, 7.9%.

In the same vein, Orliac and Dillinger (2003) used a syntactic parser to extract collocations in English for inclusion in the lexicon of a English-French machine translation system. In their approach, collocation candidates are identified by considering pair of words in predicate-argument relations. Their parser is able to handle a variety of syntactic constructions (e.g. active, passive, infinitive and gerundive constructions), but cannot deal with relative constructions. In an experiment that evaluated the extraction coverage, the relative constructions have been found responsible for nearly half of the candidate pairs missed by the collocation extraction system.

Another substantial work in the same direction was performed by Villada Moirón (2005), who experimented with syntax-based collocation extraction approaches for Dutch. The author used a parser to extract preposition-noun-preposition collocations from corpora. Sentences longer than 20 words were excluded, since they were problematic for the parser. Because of the numerous PP-attachment errors, the parser precision was not high enough to allow for the accurate detection of collocations of the above-mentioned collocation type. Therefore, the author adopted an alternative approach, based on partial parsing.

In the context of a long-standing language analysis project at the University of Geneva, we developed the first broad-coverage syntax-based extractor (Seretan and Wehrli, 2006; Seretan, 2008, 2011).[7] Initially available for English and French, it was later extended to other languages (Spanish, Italian, Greek, Romanian) and used for lexical resource development. As mentioned earlier, we adopted a fully syntactically motivated approach to collocation extraction, considering that the first extraction stage, candidate selection, is the most important one. This was in contrast to mainstream approaches, which paid more attention to candidate ranking than to the quality of the candidate dataset.

In our extractor, collocation candidates are identified as pairs of syntactically related words in predefined syntactic relations, such as the ones listed in Hausmann's definition (see Sect. 2). Our extraction is able to detect collocation candidates even if they occur in very complex syntactic environments. This is illustrated by the example below, in which the candidate *submit proposal* is identified in spite of the intervening relative clause:

(1) A joint *proposal* which addressed such elements as notification, consultations, conciliation and mediation, arbitration, panel procedures, technical assistance, adoption of panel reports and GATTs surveillance of their implementation was *submitted* on behalf of fourteen participants.

We comparatively evaluated the performance of syntax-based extraction and window-based extraction in a series of experiments. For instance, in an experiment involving a stratified sample (i.e. pairs extracted at various levels in the output list, from the top to 10%), the extraction precision was found to rise on average per language from 33.2% to 88.8% in terms of grammaticality and from 17.2% to 43.2% in terms of lexicographic interest of the results. The recall was measured in several case studies, which revealed relative strength and weaknesses of the syntax-based and syntax-free approaches. In one such study, it was found that relative to the number of collocation instances identified in a French corpus by the two methods

[7] The extraction system was named FipsCo, as it relies on the output of the Fips parser (Laenzlinger and Wehrli, 1991; Wehrli, 1997; Wehrli and Nerima, 2015). It is available online at http://latlapps.unige.ch (accessed 1 February 2018).

in total (198 instances), the window method identified 70.2% and the syntax-based method 98%.

The example below shows an instance that is missed by the syntax-based method (*payer impôt*, 'pay tax'), because of a semantically transparent noun (*partie*, 'part') intervening on the syntactic path between the verb and the object.

(2) qui *paient* déjà la majeure **partie** des *impôts*
'that already *pay* the biggest **part** of the *taxes*'

These recall-related deficiencies are however largely outweighed by the almost perfect precision of the results. Moreover, by drastically reducing the pool of candidates generated, the syntax-based approach makes it possible to extend the extraction in directions that are underexplored because of the combinatorial explosion problem. One of the extensions considered was, for instance, the iterative application of the collocation procedure in order to detect collocations of unrestricted length, such as *take [a] decisive step*, *take [a] bold decisive step* and so on (Seretan et al., 2003).

A limitation of our approach, which we recently overcame, was the identification of verbal collocations in which the nominal argument is pronominalised (cf. Example 3). The syntactic parser was extended to incorporate an anaphora resolution module, which links the pronominal argument of the verb to its antecedent (Wehrli et al., to appear). Thanks to this module, the new version of the extractor is able to retrieve the nominal collocate (*money*) and to link it to the verbal base (*spend*), even if it occurs in a previous sentence.

(3) Lots of EU *money* are owing to Poland and the rest. *It* must be *spent* fast.

This example illustrates the performance achieved by a collocation extraction pipeline that integrates advanced language analysis modules, such as syntactic parsing and anaphora resolution.

4 Using Collocations (and Other Multi-word Expressions) for Parsing

Collocational analysis is performed in order to improve knowledge about words in general and about complex lexical items (phraseology) in particular. Knowledge about lexical items – the units of language – is at the cornerstone of any language application. Phraseological knowledge has been shown to lead to improvements in the performance of a large number of NLP tasks and applications, including POS tagging and parsing, word sense disambiguation, information extraction, information retrieval, paraphrase recognition, question answering and sentiment analysis (Monti et al., 2018).

As far as syntactic parsing is concerned, the literature provides significant evidence for the positive impact of integrating phraseological knowledge, including collocations, into parsing systems. For instance, Brun (1998) showed that by using a glossary of complex nominal units in the preprocessing component of a parser, the number of parsing alternatives is significantly reduced. Similarly, Nivre and Nilsson (2004) studied the impact that the pre-recognition of phraseological units has on a Swedish parser. They reported a significant improvement in parsing accuracy and coverage when the parser is trained on a treebank in which phraseological units are treated as single tokens. Zhang and Kordoni (2006) used a similar 'words-with-spaces' pre-recognition approach and reported improvements in the coverage of an English parser. A significant increase in coverage was also observed by Villavicencio et al. (2007) when they added phraseological knowledge into the lexicon of their parser. The same 'words-with-spaces' approach was found by Korkontzelos and Manandhar (2010) to increase in the accuracy of shallow parsing of nominal compound and proper nouns. Finally, reports from the PARSEME[8] community also confirmed that the pre-recognition of complex lexical items has a positive impact on both parsing accuracy and efficiency, the parsing search space being substantially reduced when analyses compatible with complex lexical items are promoted (Constant and Sigogne, 2011; Constant et al., 2012).

These reports prove that information on lexical combinatorics is useful in guiding parsing attachments, especially in 'words-with-spaces' pre-recognition approaches, in which complex lexical items are treated as single tokens. But these approaches have two major shortcomings:

- they are not suitable to syntactically flexible items, which are the most numerous of all phraseological units (with the exception of rigid compounds like *by and large*);
- by imposing a predefined structure for the analysis of a complex lexical item, they take an early commitment on the parsing strategy, which may be wrong and compromise the analysis of the context sentence.

An example illustrating the second point is provided below. The first sentence contains an instance of the verb-object collocation *ask question*. In the second sentence, the same combination *question asked* is in a subject-verb syntactic relation. Treating it as a verb-object collocation leads the parser on a wrong path.

(4a) Any *question asked* during the selection and interview process must be related to the job and the performance of that job.
(4b) The *question asked* if the grant funding could be used as start-up capital to develop this project.

When attempting to couple syntactic and collocational analysis, a further complication that arises is the interdependency between the two types of analysis:

[8]PARSEME (2013–2017) was a European COST Action focusing on the link between complex lexical items and a comprehensive linguistic analysis of text. With more than 200 members from 33 countries, the Action fostered research on the integration of complex lexical items in parsing and translation.

we need collocational knowledge for parsing, but we need parsing to acquire collocational knowledge from corpora. To break this deadlock, we proposed a synergetic approach for the two tasks, namely, collocation identification and parsing attachment decision (Wehrli et al., 2010).

In this approach, the existing collocation information is taken into account during parsing in order to give preference to attachments involving collocation items, but without, however, making a definitive (possibly risky) commitment. Parsing and collocational analysis go hand in hand in a combined analysis, with no necessity to wait for the results of each analysis.

We evaluated this approach by comparing two versions of the parser, one with and the other without synergetic processing. The evaluation showed that the synergetic approach leads to an increase in the parser performance in terms of coverage while at the same time producing an increase in the collocation identification performance.

5 Conclusion

In this chapter, we explored the relationship between syntactic parsing and collocation extraction. Both tasks are essential for (computer-based) language understanding; both have been extensively addressed by the corresponding research communities, and significant advances have been made on each side. But, paradoxically, communication between the two was only rarely considered. Despite the development of fast and robust parsers for an increasing number of languages, collocation extraction work remains mostly focused on improving candidate ranking methods, instead of candidate selection methods – a situation which leads to the perpetration of the 'garbage in, garbage out' principle and its effects. And, despite the development of collocational resources, syntactic parsing work still lacks (in general) appropriate ways to exploit these resources for improving parsing decisions. The integration of knowledge about complex lexical items is still confined, in parsing and translation, to 'words-with-spaces' approaches. These are appropriate for rigid items but fully inappropriate for collocations, which are morphosyntactically flexible and therefore cannot be treated as single tokens.

Our chapter focused on the few exceptional works, which did take into account the advances made in one area in order to foster the other area and vice versa. We reviewed the most representative collocation extraction work which relied on syntactic parsing (or at least highlighted the need for parsing in the area of collocation extraction). We also reviewed some of the few works on syntactic parsing that exploited collocational information for parsing. These are bricks laid at the end of the bridge that aims to fill the gap between the two sides. Even though the research community has made particular efforts to unite the two ends, the bridge is not yet complete. We expect future years to bring exciting new developments in this direction and thus to enable better communication between the two research communities and, ultimately, to improve language understanding, thanks to converging language analysis efforts.

Acknowledgements I am grateful to the anonymous reviewers, whose comments and suggestions allowed me to improve the chapter.

References

Breidt, E. (1993). Extraction of V-N-collocations from text corpora: A feasibility study for German. In *Proceedings of the Workshop on Very Large Corpora: Academic and Industrial Perspectives*, Columbus (pp. 74–83).

Brun, C. (1998). Terminology finite-state preprocessing for computational LFG. In *Proceedings of the 36th Annual Meeting of the Association for Computational Linguistics and 17th International Conference on Computational Linguistics*, Morristown (pp. 196–200).

Charest, S., Brunelle, E., Fontaine, J., & Pelletier, B. (2007). Élaboration automatique d'un dictionnaire de cooccurrences grand public. In *Actes de la 14e conférence sur le Traitement Automatique des Langues Naturelles (TALN 2007)*, Toulouse (pp. 283–292).

Choueka, Y. (1988). Looking for needles in a haystack, or locating interesting collocational expressions in large textual databases. In *Proceedings of the International Conference on User-Oriented Content-Based Text and Image Handling*, Cambridge, MA (pp. 609–623).

Church, K., & Hanks, P. (1990). Word association norms, mutual information, and lexicography. *Computational Linguistics, 16*(1), 22–29.

Constant, M., & Sigogne, A. (2011). MWU-aware part-of-speech tagging with a CRF model and lexical resources. In *Proceedings of the Workshop on Multiword Expressions: From Parsing and Generation to the Real World* (pp. 49–56). Portland: Association for Computational Linguistics.

Constant, M., Sigogne, A., & Watrin, P. (2012). Discriminative strategies to integrate multiword expression recognition and parsing. In *Proceedings of the 50th Annual Meeting of the Association for Computational Linguistics (Volume 1: Long Papers)* (pp. 204–212). Jeju Island: Association for Computational Linguistics.

Daille, B. (1994). Approche mixte pour l'extraction automatique de terminologie: Statistiques lexicales et filtres linguistiques. Ph.D. thesis, Université Paris 7.

Dunning, T. (1993). Accurate methods for the statistics of surprise and coincidence. *Computational Linguistics, 19*(1), 61–74.

Evert, S. (2004). The statistics of word cooccurrences: Word pairs and collocations. Ph.D. thesis, University of Stuttgart.

Evert, S., & Krenn, B. (2005). Using small random samples for the manual evaluation of statistical association measures. *Computer Speech & Language, 19*(4), 450–466.

Gross, M. (1984). Lexicon-grammar and the syntactic analysis of French. In *Proceedings of the 10th Annual Computational Linguistics and 22nd Meeting of the Association for Computational Linguistics*, Morristown. (pp. 275–282).

Hausmann, F. J. (1989). Le dictionnaire de collocations. In F. Hausmann, O. Reichmann, H. Wiegand, & L. Zgusta (Eds.), *Wörterbücher: Ein internationales Handbuch zur Lexicographie* (pp. 1010–1019). Berlin: Dictionaries, Dictionnaires, de Gruyter.

Hornby, A. S., Cowie, A. P., & Lewis, J. W. (1948). *Oxford advanced learner'dictionary of current English*. London: Oxford University Press.

Huang, C. R., Kilgarriff, A., Wu, Y., Chiu, C. M., Smith, S., Rychly, P., Bai, M. H., & Chen, K. J. (2005). Chinese sketch engine and the extraction of grammatical collocations. In *Proceedings of the Fourth SIGHAN Workshop on Chinese Language Processing*, Jeju Island (pp. 48–55).

Kilgarriff, A., Rychly, P., Smrz, P., & Tugwell, D. (2004). The sketch engine. In *Proceedings of the Eleventh EURALEX International Congress*, Lorient (pp. 105–116).

Korkontzelos, I., & Manandhar, S. (2010). Can recognising multiword expressions improve shallow parsing? In *Human Language Technologies: The 2010 Annual Conference of the North American Chapter of the Association for Computational Linguistics* (pp. 636–644). Los Angeles: Association for Computational Linguistics.

Krenn, B. (2000). Collocation mining: Exploiting corpora for collocation identification and representation. In *Proceedings of the KONVENS 2000*, Ilmenau (pp. 209–214).

Laenzlinger, C., & Wehrli, E. (1991). Fips, un analyseur interactif pour le français. *TA Informations, 32*(2), 35–49.

Lafon, P. (1984). *Dépouillements et statistiques en lexicométrie*. Genève/Paris: Slatkine – Champion.

Lea, D., & Runcie, M. (Eds.). (2002). *Oxford collocations dictionary for students of English*. Oxford: Oxford University Press.

Lin, D. (1998). Extracting collocations from text corpora. In *Proceedings of the First Workshop on Computational Terminology*, Montreal (pp. 57–63).

Lin, D. (1999). Automatic identification of non-compositional phrases. In *Proceedings of the 37th Annual Meeting of the Association for Computational Linguistics on Computational Linguistics*, Morristown (pp. 317–324).

Lü, Y., & Zhou, M. (2004). Collocation translation acquisition using monolingual corpora. In *Proceedings of the 42nd Meeting of the Association for Computational Linguistics (ACL'04)*, Barcelona (pp. 167–174)

Mel'čuk, I. (2003). Collocations: Définition, rôle et utilité. In F. Grossmann, & A. Tutin (Eds.), *Les collocations: Analyse et traitement* (pp. 23–32). Amsterdam: Editions De Werelt

Monti, J., Seretan, V., Pastor, G. C., & Mitkov, R. (2018). Multiword units in machine translation and translation technology. In R. Mitkov, J. Monti, G. C. Pastor, & V. Seretan (Eds.), *Multiword units in machine translation and translation technology* (Current issues in linguistic theory, Vol. 341). Amsterdam/Philadelphia: John Benjamins.

Nivre, J. (2006). *Inductive dependency parsing (Text, speech and language technology)*. Secaucus: Springer.

Nivre, J., & Nilsson, J. (2004). Multiword units in syntactic parsing. In *MEMURA 2004 – Methodologies and Evaluation of Multiword Units in Real-World Applications (LREC Workshop)* (pp. 39–46).

Nugues, P. M. (2014). *Corpus processing tools* (pp. 23–64). Berlin/Heidelberg: Springer.

Orliac, B., & Dillinger, M. (2003). Collocation extraction for machine translation. In *Proceedings of Machine Translation Summit IX*, New Orleans (pp. 292–298).

Pearce, D. (2001). Synonymy in collocation extraction. In *Proceedings of the NAACL Workshop on WordNet and Other Lexical Resources: Applications, Extensions and Customizations*, Pittsburgh (pp. 41–46).

Pearce, D. (2002). A comparative evaluation of collocation extraction techniques. In *Third International Conference on Language Resources and Evaluation*, Las Palmas (pp. 1530–1536).

Pecina, P. (2005). An extensive empirical study of collocation extraction methods. In *Proceedings of the ACL Student Research Workshop*, Ann Arbor (pp. 13–18).

Pecina, P. (2008). Lexical association measures: Collocation extraction. Ph.D. thesis, Charles University.

Piao, S. S., Rayson, P., Archera, D., & McEnery, T. (2005). Comparing and combining a semantic tagger and a statistical tool for MWE extraction. *Computer Speech and Language Special Issue on Multiword Expressions, 19*(4), 378–397.

Rani, A., Mehla, K., & Jangra, A. (2015). Parsers and parsing approaches: Classification and state of the art. In *Proceedings of the 2015 International Conference on Futuristic Trends on Computational Analysis and Knowledge Management (ABLAZE)*, New Delhi (pp. 34–38).

Sag, I. A., Baldwin, T., Bond, F., Copestake, A., & Flickinger, D. (2002). Multiword expressions: A pain in the neck for NLP. In *Proceedings of the Third International Conference on Intelligent Text Processing and Computational Linguistics (CICLING 2002)*, Mexico City (pp. 1–15).

Seretan, V. (2008). Collocation extraction based on syntactic parsing. Ph.D. thesis, University of Geneva.

Seretan, V. (2011). *Syntax-based collocation extraction, text, speech and language technology* (Vol. 44). Dordrecht: Springer.

Seretan, V., & Wehrli, E. (2006). Accurate collocation extraction using a multilingual parser. In *Proceedings of the 21st International Conference on Computational Linguistics and 44th Annual Meeting of the Association for Computational Linguistics*, Sydney (pp. 953–960).

Seretan, V., Nerima, L., & Wehrli, E. (2003). Extraction of multi-word collocations using syntactic bigram composition. In *Proceedings of the Fourth International Conference on Recent Advances in NLP (RANLP-2003)*, Borovets (pp. 424–431).

Shimohata, S., Sugio, T., & Nagata, J. (1997). Retrieving collocations by co-occurrences and word order constraints. In *Proceedings of the Annual Meeting of the Association for Computational Linguistics*, Madrid (pp. 476–481).

Sinclair, J. (1995). *Collins cobuild english dictionary*. London: Harper Collins.

Smadja, F. (1993). Retrieving collocations from text: Xtract. *Computational Linguistics, 19*(1), 143–177.

Tzoukermann, E., & Radev, D. R. (1996). Using word class for part-of-speech disambiguation. In *Proceedings of the Fourth Workshop on Very Large Corpora*, Copenhagen (pp. 1–13).

Uhrig, P., & Proisl, T. (2012). Less hay, more needles – using dependency-annotated corpora to provide lexicographers with more accurate lists of collocation candidates. *Lexicographica, 28*(1), 141–180.

Villada Moirón, M. B. (2005). Data-driven identification of fixed expressions and their modifiability. Ph.D. thesis, University of Groningen.

Villavicencio, A., Kordoni, V., Zhang, Y., Idiart, M., & Ramisch, C. (2007). Validation and evaluation of automatically acquired multiword expressions for grammar engineering. In *Proceedings of the 2007 Joint Conference on Empirical Methods in Natural Language Processing and Computational Natural Language Learning (EMNLP-CoNLL)*, Prague (pp. 1034–1043).

Wehrli, E. (1997). *L'analyse syntaxique des langues naturelles: Problèmes et méthodes*. Paris: Masson.

Wehrli, E., & Nerima, L. (2015). The fips multilingual parser. In N. Gala, R. Rapp, & G. Bel-Enguix (Eds.), *Language production, cognition, and the lexicon, text, speech and language technology* (Vol. 48, pp. 473–489). Cham: Springer.

Wehrli, E., Seretan, V., & Nerima, L. (2010). Sentence analysis and collocation identification. In *Proceedings of the Workshop on Multiword Expressions: From Theory to Applications (MWE 2010)*, Beijing (pp. 27–35).

Wehrli, E., Seretan, V., & Nerima, L. (to appear) Verbal collocations and pronominalization. In G. C. Pastor & U. Heid (Eds.), *Currrent trends in computational phraseology, research in linguistics and literature*. Amsterdam/Philadelphia: John Benjamins.

Wu, H., & Zhou, M. (2003). Synonymous collocation extraction using translation information. In *Proceeding of the Annual Meeting of the Association for Computational Linguistics (ACL 2003)*, Sapporo (pp. 120–127).

Zhang, Y., & Kordoni, V. (2006). Automated deep lexical acquisition for robust open texts processing. In *Proceedings of LREC-2006*, Genoa (pp. 275–280).

Chapter 3
Network Analysis Techniques Applied to Dictionaries for Identifying Semantics in Lexical Spanish Collocations

Isabel Sánchez-Berriel, Octavio Santana Suárez, Virginia Gutiérrez Rodríguez, and José Pérez Aguiar

Abstract The definitions in dictionaries are a source of information to support the results obtained by the automatic extraction of collocations from a text corpus. Measures of association, which are generally used in this task, are useful tools to extract candidate combinations. However, they do not offer information about other features of the collocations. They do not distinguish whether a combination is categorized as a collocation because of its frequency properties or because of its structural properties. Moreover, they cannot distinguish between *lexical collocations* and *functional collocations* with delexicalized elements. In this paper, we use a graph database for representing collocations and relations between words retrieved from dictionaries. We consider relations between lemmas and *definiens* in dictionary entries as well as relations between two words used to define the same sense of another one. This allows us to use a clustering algorithm and measures of centrality and influence in networks to identify semantic characteristics of combinations. The aim is to enrich the information on the combinatorial restrictions of words based on frequencies obtained by means of corpus linguistic techniques.

1 Introduction

There are two main conceptions of collocation in the literature: a statistical one and a linguistic one (Hausmann and Blumenthal 2006; Siepmann 2005). The former represents collocation as a recurrent combination of words or word forms. Techniques from statistic or from information theory have usually been used for automatic detection of these patterns in a textual corpus (Church & Hanks 1999).

I. Sánchez-Berriel (✉) · V. G. Rodríguez
Universidad de La Laguna, Tenerife, Spain
e-mail: isanchez@ull.edu.es

O. S. Suárez · J. P. Aguiar
Universidad de Las Palmas de Gran Canaria, Canaria, Spain

P. Cantos-Gómez, M. Almela-Sánchez (eds.), *Lexical Collocation Analysis*, Quantitative Methods in the Humanities and Social Sciences,
https://doi.org/10.1007/978-3-319-92582-0_3

Some of them are mutual information, z-score, t-score, log Dice, etc. They are computed from the combination frequencies and word frequencies in the analyzed texts (Evert 2005). These word association measures are useful for compiling lists of lexical combinations commonly used in the language.

In contrast, the linguistic or qualitative approach to the concept of collocation represents it as a lexically and structurally restricted combination of words in which one of the elements is semantically dependent on the other. For example, we assign the meaning of "intense flavor" to the adjective *fuerte* when it is used with the noun *café* to form the "café fuerte" (*strong coffee*) collocation. Statistical measures of lexical association have only a limited applicability in the identification and description of these expressions. The relationship between the elements of a restricted collocation is more complex than the typicality. The main problems encountered are the following ones:

- Not all frequent combinations are collocations in the narrow sense of the term.
- Low-frequency combinations can form part of restricted collocations.
- Frequency parameters are insufficient to detect semantic properties present in the collocations (Bartsch 2004; Wanner et al. 2016).
- In general, the association is established with semantic groups formed by more than one lexeme (Bosque 2004b):

  Sp. terminantemente *(strictly-flatly)* + verbs that denote rejection or denial {prohibir, negar, desmentir, excluir, rechazar, etc.} *({prohibit, negate, deny, exclude, reject,* etc.*})*

  universalmente *(universally)* + verbs that denote acceptance {aprobar, aceptar, admitir, acatar, etc.} *({approve, accept, admit, obey, comply with,* etc.*})*
- Most measures of association are symmetrical, i.e. they do not allow differentiation in the direction of predictability – for an exception, see Gries' Delta P (2013). For example, in *medida drástica (drastic measure)*, there is a greater possibility that the adjective *drástico (drastic)* appears in the context of *medida* (*measure*) than *medida* (*measure*) appears with *drástico*. In any case, not all the directional properties of collocations can be captured by means of association measures, since some of these properties are inherently qualitative (particularly the semantic and the lexical dependency of one of the elements).

This paper describes different strategies for the automatic treatment of dictionary definitions in order to complement the statistical rankings of word combinations. The objective will be focused on *functional collocations* of noun + verb, like Sp. *tener miedo* (*to be afraid*), in which the collocate *tener* is delexicalized and functions as a support verb of the base: *miedo*. The properties of these collocations will be distinguished from those of *lexical collocations*.

In the next section, we will provide a brief description of semantic and grammatical aspects of different types of Spanish collocations. In Sect. 3, we address the potential of dictionary definitions as a source of information for collocation extraction and classification. Section 4 explains the characteristics of the dataset employed in this study. Section 5 deals with graph databases and explains the reasons why they have been chosen as data models in this research. In Sect. 6 some techniques of graph analysis are presented, with special emphasis on their contribution as a complement of association measures. Section 7 offers some conclusions.

2 Spanish Collocations

Studies on Spanish collocations began in the 1990s, although in the late 1970s, Seco (1978, 1979) had referred to the term *collocation* (Corpas Pastor 1996; Penadés Martínez 2001; Castillo Carballo 1998). Corpas Pastor (1996) considers them a type of phraseological units. Bosque (2001, 2004b) analyzes them as manifestations of the restrictions that predicates impose on the selection of their arguments. He observes that collocates select lexical classes and not just individual items. For example:

> ***supino*** *selects {ignorancia, incompetencia, inutilidad, necedad, desconocimiento, estupidez, ridiculez, imbecilidad, irresponsabilidad, egoísmo, cinismo} ({ignorance, incompetence, uselessness, foolishness, stupidity, ridiculousness, imbecility, irresponsibility, selfishness, cynicism})*

In meaning-text theory, *lexical functions* (Table 3.1) are used to represent common relationships between lexemes in collocations (Alonso Ramos 2002b; Mel'čuk 1998). Nevertheless, there are collocations that cannot be described by means of lexical functions. A case in point is *discusión bizantina* (*pointless argument*) (Koike 2001).

The question of what constitutes a collocation is a controversial one. There are discrepancies among authors regarding that exact criteria by which a given combination should be classified as a collocation. For example, the following cases may be controversial Bosque (2001):

> *ejecutar un castigo (to mete out a punishment)*
> *empantanarse un proyecto (a project gets bogged down)*
> *enfilar la calle principal (to go straight along the main street)*
> *disminución progresiva (gradual decrease)*

It is generally, though not unanimously, agreed that collocations occupy an intermediate area between free combinations and idioms. On the one hand, collocations exhibit formal flexibility, a characteristic that distinguishes them from fixed expressions and idioms (Koike 2001). Proof of this is the fact that they

Table 3.1 Lexical functions examples

Lexical function	Semantic	Example	
Magn	*Very, intense*	Magn(*enemigo*) = *acérrimo*	(*Bitter enemy*)
Mult	*Whole*	Mult(*oveja*) = *rebaño*	(*Flock of sheep*)
Sing	*Portion*	Sing(*pan*) = *rebanada*	(*Slice of bread*)

allow for variable grammatical categories, modification by means of adjectives, transformation to passive, relativization, nominalization, and pronominalization.

comida frugal (frugal food)/comer frugalmente (to eat frugally)
hacer un aterrizaje (to make a landing)/hacer un aterrizaje forzoso (to make an emergency landing)
trasplantar órganos (to transplant organs)/el órgano fue transplantado (the organ was transplanted)

On the other hand, collocations are also distinguished from free combinations by the dependent status of one of the components. Collocations are asymmetrical structures consisting of a *base* (Fr. *base*, Germ. *Basis*, Sp. *base*) and a *collocate* (Fr. *collocatif*, Germ. *Kollokatif*, Sp. *colocativo*) (Hausmann 1979; Mel'čuk 1998). The base is semantically autonomous, but the collocate is dependent on the base (this use of the term *collocate* should not be confused with the concept of *collocate* in the Firthian tradition, where it refers to frequent lexical co-occurrence). This dependency is manifested in several ways, including the presence of the base as an essential feature in the definition of the collocate, the delexicalization of the collocate, or the selection of a special – often figurative – sense in the collocate. As an example of the latter, we can mention *banco de peces* (*shoal of fish*), *precio astronómico* (*astronomical price*), and *levantar sesión* (*to end session*). The collocates in these examples are underlined, and their definitions in the *Diccionario de la Lengua Española* (2017; DLE, hereafter) are shown below. In all these combinations, the presence of the base resolves the ambiguity of the collocate.

banco. 5. m. Conjunto de peces que van juntos en gran número.
astronómico. 2. adj. coloq. Que se considera desmesuradamente grande. Sumas, distancias astronómicas.
sesión. levantar la ~**.** Concluirla

In other cases, the collocate has a very specific and stable meaning which is determined by the specialization of its use in the context of the base. Some cases in point are *triángulo isósceles* (*isosceles triangle*), *la abeja querocha* (*bee lays eggs*), *pelo lacio* (*straight hair*), *el barco zarpa* (*the boat sets sail*), and *trinchar carne* (*to carve meat*). In these examples, the collocates are terms for specific properties, actions, or processes of the bases, and there is a typical link between both. Thus, *isosceles* describes a type of *triangle*, *querochar* refers to an activity performed by bees, *lacio* is a quality attributed to the hair, and so on (see DLE 2017 definitions below).

isósceles. v. triángulo isósceles
querochar. 1. intr. Dicho de las abejas y de otros insectos: Poner la querocha.
lacio, cia. 3. Dicho del cabello: Que cae sin formar ondas ni rizos.
zarpar. **2.** intr. Dicho de un barco o de un conjunto de ellos: Salir del lugar en que estaban fondeados o atracados.
trinchar. **1.** Partir en trozos la comida para servirla.

From a grammatical point of view, Koike (2001) classifies Spanish collocations into the following groups: noun + verb, adjective + noun, noun + *de* + noun, verb

Table 3.2 Grammatical typology of Spanish collocations according Koike (2001)

	Base	Example
Noun + verb	Noun	*correr un rumor (rumor spreads)* *estallar una guerra (war breaks out)* *zarpar un barco (boat sets sail)* *desempeñar un cargo (hold a post/position)* *dar comienzo (start)* *poner en cuestión (to call into question)*
Adjective + noun	Noun	*fuente fidedigna (reliable source)* *enemigo acérrimo (bitter enemy)* *oído fino (good ear)*
Noun + de + noun	Noun	*tableta de chocolate (chocolate bar)* *enjambre de abejas (swarm of bees)*
Verb + adverb	Verb	*caer pesadamente (to fall heavily)* *negar rotundamente (to flatly refuse)*
Adverb + adjective/participle	Adjective	*firmemente convencido (firmly convinced)* *rematadamente loco (utterly crazy)*
Verb + adjective	Adjective	*resultar ileso (to be unhurt)* *salir malparado (to come off badly)*

Table 3.3 Functional collocations verb + noun

Functional noun + verb	Related verb	
tener miedo	*temer*	(*To be afraid*)
hacer una aclaración	*aclarar*	(*To clarify*)
dar un golpe	*golpear*	(*To hit*)
albergar esperanza	*esperar*	(*To cherish*)

+ adverb, and verb + adjective (Table 3.2). There are also complex collocations in which one of the collocates can be a nominal, adjectival, or adverbial phrase.

In this study, we have focused on simple collocations, namely, on two of the aforementioned grammatical categories, highlighted by Koike (2001), for being particularly frequent and due to their communicative relevance in Spanish: noun + verb and adjective + noun.

More specifically, verb-noun collocations have been classified into two groups, according to their semantic properties: *functional collocations* and *lexical collocations* (Koike 2001; Molina-Plaza and Sancho-Guinda 2007; Jiménez Martínez 2016). In functional collocations, the collocate is a support verb. It is semantically empty or has a highly schematic meaning (Table 3.3). In these combinations, the noun conveys the core lexical meaning, and the verb contributes information about number, person, tense, and aspect. In many cases, there is a simple verb morphologically related to the noun (Koike 1993):

In contrast, lexical verbs form lexical collocations. Koike (2001) distinguished two types of lexical collocations, depending on whether the accompanying noun is concrete or abstract. Verb (lexical) + (concrete) noun results into lexical collocates in those instances whenever the verb conveys a typical relationship with the concrete noun (Table 3.5). This explains why *tocar la guitarra (to play the guitar)* is a lexical collocate but *comprar una guitarra (to buy a guitar)* is not. Furthermore, verbs

Table 3.4 Functional collocations noun + adjective

Functional noun + adjective
error garrafal (terrible mistake)
módico precio (reasonable price)
dolor atroz (terrible pain)
comida atroz (terrible, awful food)
tiempo horroroso (terrible weather)
chico fenomenal (amazing, great boy/guy)

Table 3.5 Lexical collocations

Noun + verb	Noun + adjective
moler café (to grind coffee)	*pelo lacio (straight hair)*
zarpar barco (to set sail)	*barrio céntrico (center of town)*
amasar fortuna (to amass fortune)	*cuchillo afilado (sharp knife)*
afrontar riesgo (to amass fortune)	*gobierno autoritario (authoritarian government)*

Table 3.6 Collocations in the outline of the definition (DGLE)

Definition	Collocation
arriar: Bajar [una vela o bandera que estaba izada]	*arriar vela, bandera (to lower sail, a flag)*
enarbolar Levantar en alto [estandarte, bandera, etc.]	*enarbolar estandarte, bandera (to hoist banner, flag)*
vibrar: Agitar en el aire [la pica, la lanza, etc.]; arrojar con ímpetu y violencia [una cosa que vibre]	*vibrar pica, lanza (to vibrate a lance, spear)*
suspender: especialmente, figurado. Privar temporalmente [a uno del sueldo o empleo] que tenía	*suspender sueldo, empleo (to suspend salary, employment)*

(lexical) + abstract nouns are less likely to form lexical collocations and are more prone to result into functional ones.

The second simple collocation we have considered in this research is adjective + noun. This grammatical category allows also the constructions of both: lexical and functional collocations (Koike 2001). In those co-occurrences where the adjective has a quantitative or qualitative intensifier role, we get functional collocations (Table 3.4): *buena salud (good health)* or *tiempo horroroso (dreadful weather)*. Instead, semantically positive marked adjectives and nouns form lexical collocations (Table 3.5): *recuerdo grato (fond memory)* or *crítica favorable (positive feedback)*.

The constituents in a lexical collocation keep their full meaning, and the meaning of the whole collocation is completely compositional.

3 Collocations in Spanish Dictionaries

Information about Spanish collocations has been encoded in different types of dictionaries. The *Diccionario de Colocaciones del Español* (DICE; Alonso 2002b) describes combinatorial restrictions of lexemes by means of lexical functions

(Alonso Ramos 2002a; Vincze 2011; Vincze and Alonso Ramos 2013). The dictionaries *Redes* and *Diccionario Combinatorio Práctico del Español Contemporáneo* (Bosque 2004a, 2006) provide systematic descriptions of lexical classes whose members co-occur with a given collocate. In addition, information about combinatorial restrictions of words is also found in traditional dictionaries. In the *Diccionario del Español Actual* (DEA; Seco et al. 1992) and in the *Diccionario General de la Lengua Española* (DGLE; 2008), the outline of the definition is specified by brackets. The outline of a definition specifies the semantic type (or types) to which the characteristics expressed by a predicative lexeme apply. As Bosque (2004b) observed, almost all the definitional outlines ("contornos lexicográficos") form semantic restrictions imposed on the arguments of a particular predicate.

In general, when the *definiendum* is a collocate, the outline corresponds to the base. If the collocate is an adjective, this is expressed by means of definitional formulae such as *Dicho normalmente de*, *Referido esp. a*, etc. (Table 3.6).

If the outline describes general features, not all the words that contain them will necessarily form a collocation with the *definiendum* (see Table 3.4: definitions vs. collocations).

Often, the definitions of denominal verbs make use of functional collocations (see Table 3.7). As for the adjectives, the collocations are observed in the outline (see Table 3.8).

Table 3.7 Functional collocations in the definition of denominal verbs

Definition	Collocation
desesperanzar: Quitar la esperanza [a uno]	*quitar esperanza (to remove all hope)*
esperanzar: Dar esperanza [a uno]	*dar esperanza (to give hope)*
esperanzar: Tener esperanza	*tener esperanza (to hope)*
apasionar: Llenarse de pasión	*llenarse de pasión (to be filled with passion)*
apasionar: Causar, excitar alguna pasión [a uno]	*causar pasión (to arouse passion)*
respetar: Tener respeto	*tener respeto (to have respect)*

Table 3.8 Collocations adjective + noun from its outline

Definition	Collocation
acéfalo: [sociedad, secta, etc.] Que no tiene jefe	*sociedad, secta acéfala (leaderless society, sect)*
acéfalo: [feto] Sin cabeza o sin parte considerable de ella	*feto acéfalo (headless fetus)*
frío: por extensión. [color] Que produce efectos sedantes como el azul, el verde, etc.	*color frío (cool color)*
imberbe: [joven] Que no tiene barba	*joven imberbe (beardless boy)*
interactivo: [programa] Que permite una interacción, a modo de diálogo, entre el ordenador y el usuario	*programa interactivo (interactive program)*
recurrente: [fenómeno] Que vuelve a su punto de partida	*fenómeno recurrente recurring phenomenon*

4 Description of the Dataset

In this research we have used the Spanish lexical collocation database which supports ColexWeb (Santana et al. 2014). This database registers word frequencies and co-occurrence frequencies. The information is obtained from a collection of approximately 11,000 texts from a wide range of genres. This corpus gathers literary and nonliterary texts. The literary works are of different origins and genres: classical and contemporary, Spanish and universal, poetry and prose, theater, narrative, and essays. The literary section contains around 7758 texts. The nonliterary section contains 4108 works related to various topics: arts, biographies, science, film, Christianity, law, economics, education, esotericism, ethnology, philosophy, geography, history, linguistics, literature, politics, psychology, religion, theater criticism, and others. There is also a specific section consisting of newspaper articles. In total, the database contains approximately 300,000,000 tokens.

Due to the formal flexibility of collocations, the frequencies were calculated for combinations of canonical forms that were obtained using the *Flexionador y Lematizador de palabras del Español* of the Data Structure and Computational Linguistic Group of the University of Las Palmas de Gran Canaria (Santana et al. 1997, 1999, 2007). The collocations extracted belong to the following grammatical types: noun + verb, noun + adjective, and verb + adverb. The frequencies were obtained for these patterns, within a window size of ± 5 words and the minimum frequency threshold of 10.

The results of this processing have been stored in a database containing the frequencies of the individual canonical forms and the collocational clusters. It contains up to 6,551,979 combinations of noun + verb, 3,743,476 of noun + adjective, and 252,798 of verb + adverb. In addition, the dataset has been enriched with the values obtained from various association measures: relative frequency, z-score, t-score, and Dunning. It also incorporates a list of collocations collected from the following studies on Spanish collocations: Alonso Ramos (1994–1995), Alonso Ramos (2002a), Bosque (2001), Castillo Carballo (1997–998, 1998), Castillo Carballo (2001), Corpas Pastor (1996, 2001, 2003), García Platero (2002), García-Page (2001), and Koike (2001). Two thousand three hundred and fifty six combinations were obtained from these papers, which were then used for evaluation tasks.

Then, the database was enriched with information about the relationships between canonical forms in the definitions of the DGLE (2008). In particular, we focused on the following types of relationships: a verb in the definition of another verb, a noun in the definition of another verb, a noun marked in the outline of a verb, and a noun in the outline of an adjective. Also relevant are the number of word senses and the number of times that a verb is used to define other words. This selection is based on the following considerations:

- Delexicalized verbs are used very frequently in the definitions of the dictionary. Therefore, the number of times that a verb is used in the definitions helps us to determine whether it is likely to act as a functional verb: *dar*, *tener*, and *quitar* are verbs that correspond to this pattern.

- When there is a functional verb in the definition, the semantic precision required to define another verb is provided by the collocation with a noun. This allows us to establish functional collocations: *dar confianza* (*to give confidence*) and *tener respeto* (*to have respect*) are examples of collocations that instantiate this kind of relationship.
- Verbs with few senses are likely to be verbs with a specific (non-schematic) meaning. In general, verbs that can be used as support verbs are highly ambiguous.
- Verbs containing a full lexical content tend to form lexical collocations with nouns in their outline, such as *izar bandera* (*to hoist flag*).
- Combinations between verbs that have a full lexical content and general nouns such as *persona (person)*, *cosa* (*thing*), etc. are not recorded.
- Combinations of verbs and nouns with full lexical content in a dictionary definition correspond to lexical collocations:

  hechizar: *cautivar el ánimo (to captivate spirit).*
  animar: *infundir ánimo (to encourage)*

- Adjectives form collocations with the nouns that occur in their outline: *fenómeno recurrente (recurring phenomenon).*

5 Graph Database

We have analyzed associations between different lexemes by means of a graph database. In this kind of database, the data model corresponds to a graph. A graph is a set of vertices and edges, that is, a collection of nodes and relationships linking them. In the field that concerns us, the graphs represent entities as nodes and the ways in which these entities are related are called relationships, corresponding to the edges of the graph. Both nodes and relationships can have attributes, which constitute the object properties.

Most collocation extraction analyses rely on traditional software, such as WordSmith Tools (Scott 2016) and AntConc (Anthony 2018). These tools allow researchers to obtain collocates derived for a node, allowing a range of settings: measures of association, minimum frequency, the span, or the collocational strength. However, these tools/techniques force researchers to consider collocates in terms of two words at a time. In contrast, graph databases add a new dimension to collocation analysis, both theoretically and methodologically. Graph plottings enable more sophisticated analyses to be carried out which focus on links between words: networks (Baker 2016).

The notion of lexical networks is not new and dates back to Philips (1983, 1985, 1989), suggesting that words occur as networks of collocates. Furthermore, other researchers have also explored such networks (Williams 1998; Cantos and Sánchez 2001; Baker 2005, 2014; McEnery 2006; Alonso et al. 2011; Jackson and Bolger 2014; Williams et al. 2017). More recent work graphical collocations tools include *GraphColl* developed by Brezina, McEnery and Wattam (2015) to build collocation networks from user-defined corpora. *GraphColl* incorporates a number of different collocation measures, including the directional Delta P (Gries 2013). It creates graphs based on a word entered in a search box and can thus create collocation networks at any level of complexity, including first-, second-, etc. level collocations (counting from the node on).

5.1 Advantages of Using a Graph Database

The main advantage of native graph storage is due to the infrastructure of distribution that has been specially designed and built to have good performance and high scalability for processing graph models (Robinson et al. 2013). The native processing of graphs through adjacency improves the performance of queries, allowing for exploration of nodes following their relations. Compared to relational databases and other NoSQL solutions, when it comes to related data queries, this model presents an evident decrease in response time (Leavitt 2010). The performance of queries using JOIN operations in relational databases decreases as the dataset becomes larger. Each node in the graph model contains a set or list of records that represent the relationships with other nodes. These relationship records are organized by address and type and may contain attributes with additional information. This means that each time that execute operations are equivalent to a JOIN, the database uses this list of relations. Therefore, a direct access to connected nodes eliminates the need to perform an expensive search operation or matching. This ability offers a better performance, especially for heavy queries. With a graph database, the performance tends to remain relatively constant, linear, or directly proportional to the magnitude of the dataset. This is due to the fact that the queries are limited to a subset of the graph, starting its route from a node and continuing through its edges without the need to traverse a whole table or list of indexes. In this way, the execution time is proportional to the size of the subgraph concerned.

The flexibility of this model is also important since it allows adding new types of relationships, new nodes, and even new subgraphs to an existent structure, without changes in the previous queries or functionalities of the application.

Relationships themselves are the most important part of graph databases in contrast with other database systems, where the interconnections between entities use special properties such as foreign keys. Interconnections in graph database nodes and structured relationships allow us to build sophisticated models suitable to solve our problem.

6 Design of Database Schema

In this section, we expose the design decisions that have been made to represent the graph database schema of collocations. The following categories of nodes have been considered: words, nouns, verbs, adjectives, adverbs, groups, and meta-semantic groups. The relationships between nodes considered include relationships between words, relationships between a group and its meta-semantic group, and relationships between words and a group. The following lines describe each of these elements of the BD.

All nodes identified as a word will be associated with the word tag. The goal of this is to facilitate the search and distinction of words from other types. In addition, these nodes have been categorized grammatically using the following labels: noun, verb, adjective, or adverb. The properties associated with them are:

- Id: an identifier
- Form: canonical form of the word
- Category: a code for grammatical category
- Frequency: the canonical form frequency

Group represents a semantic group of words in the *Diccionario Ideológico de la Lengua Española* (Alvar 1998). It has only one identifier attribute. They are grouped into Meta-groups, which contain an attribute corresponding to the canonical form that represents its meaning. This information was retrieved from the Ideological Dictionary. To increase the performance in the execution of queries, different relationship types were generated according to the type of word in each vertex of the edge.

NOUN_TO_ADJECTIVE
NOUN_TO_VERB
VERB_TO_NOUN
ADJECTIVE_TO_NOUN
ADVERB_TO_VERB

The properties associated with the relationships between words are:

- idCollocation: identifier for the relationship between two canonical forms.
- frequencyi: combination frequency at distance i

EN_GRUPO represents the relation of belonging to a canonical form or a semantic group, and the relation EN_CABECERA, the belonging of a group to a Meta-group. Finally, the relation DEFINIDA_POR represents the association between a word and another defining it, and the type of node CONTOUR_DE is for those words that are in the outline of the definition of some other word.

This design was implemented on Neo4J, BD NoSQL, which implements the graph model efficiently at the storage level. Figure 3.1 below shows the result of a query about the final model, in which different types of nodes and relationships are seen in the Neo4J viewer. Each category of node is shown in a different color, for example, red corresponds to verbs and purple to nouns.

7 Graph of Word Analysis

The graph data model allows us to use useful techniques from network analysis to identify structures that correspond to some category of Spanish collocations: lexical or functional. In general, the graphs representing complex systems have an archi-

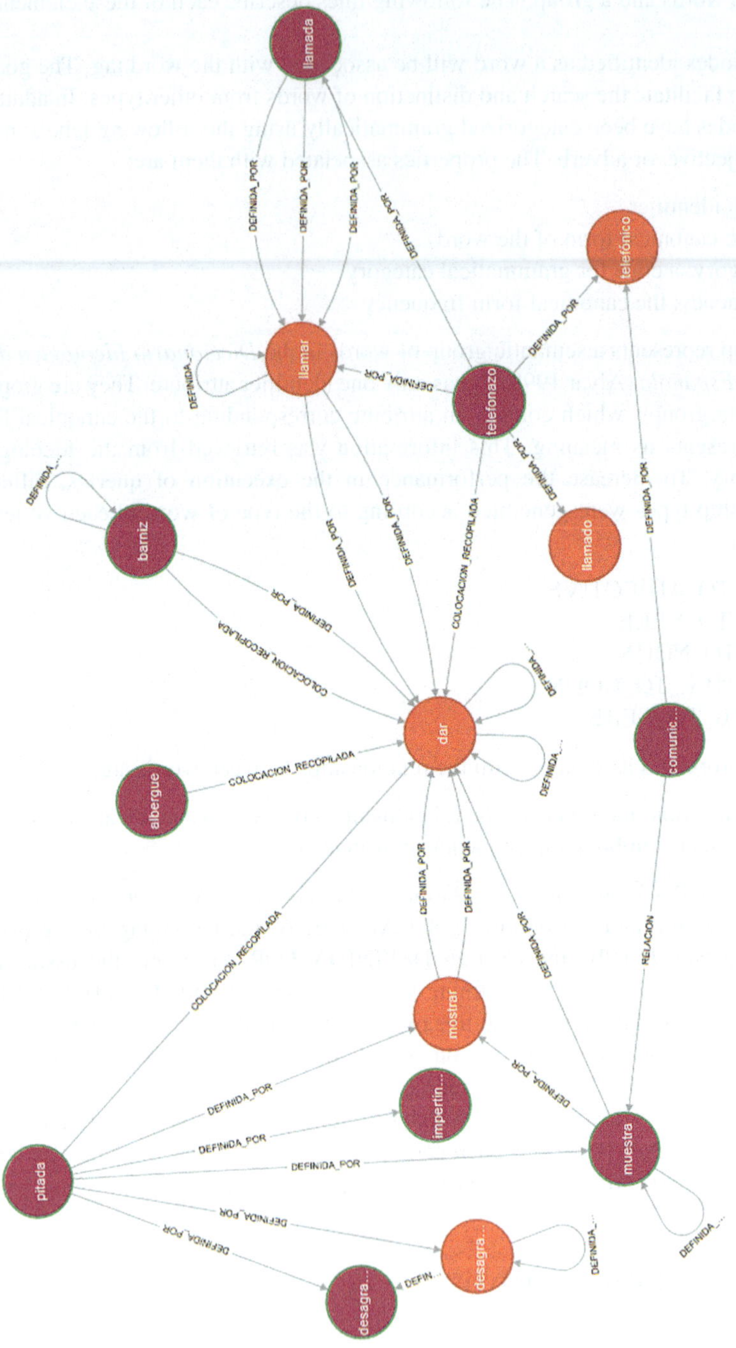

Fig. 3.1 Design of the graph database for Spanish functional associations

tecture in communities. A community in the graph is a subset of nodes with high connection density but with a low number of edges to nodes in other communities. The nodes with fewer connections usually belong to a single community and are not connected to other communities. Nodes that connect communities are called hub nodes. In the analysis of graphs, different techniques for identifying communities are defined. These techniques partition the graph into disjoint subsets. Algorithms search an optimal configuration for partition optimizing an objective function, for example, modularity. Modularity is a measure of the quality of the partition, as in Girvan-Newman algorithm. This method generates partitions successively based on a function of the intermediation. In each step, the edge with the greatest intermediation is eliminated generating subsets with fewer connections each time. Intermediation is a measure of centrality that is defined to be high in hub nodes. It measures the number of times that a node appears on the shortest path between two nodes in the network.

$$c_i = \sum_{j<k} \frac{g_{jk}(n_i)}{g_{jk}}$$

The Girvan-Newman (2002) algorithm for generating clustering consists of the following four steps:

1. Calculate the intermediation for all edges of the graph.
2. Eliminate the edge with greater intermediation.
3. Update the intermediation.
4. Repeat steps 2 and 3 until there are no edges.

Using the R package *igraph*, this algorithm has been applied to the collocational data used in the study (Kolackzyc and Csárdi 2014). It is considered that two nodes are connected if they are used together to define a word. That is, communities are determined in the network of words that form collocations that are used in the dictionary definitions, that is to say, with the relation DEFINED_FOR. The tests have been restricted to the subset of collected collocations. The network is shown below. In this network, the nodes appear with a radius proportional to the intermediation. The visualization of how the communities facilitate the identification of the type of collocations can be observed in this network. Nodes with higher values of intermediation correspond to functional verbs: *tener*, *dar*, *poner*, etc. We also see that these verbs correspond to hub nodes. Central communities with nodes of this type are formed by functional collocations. On the other hand, peripheral communities, without connection to the rest of the network, correspond to lexical collocations: *viajar barco (to travel by boat)*, *viajar autobus (to travel by bus)*, and *tocar guitarra (to play the guitar)* (Fig. 3.2).

The structure of the network in the subgraph of the noun + adjective collocations is much simpler. In this case, the hub nodes correspond to nouns (color); the adjectives are related only to a noun generating isolated sets (Figs. 3.3 and 3.4).

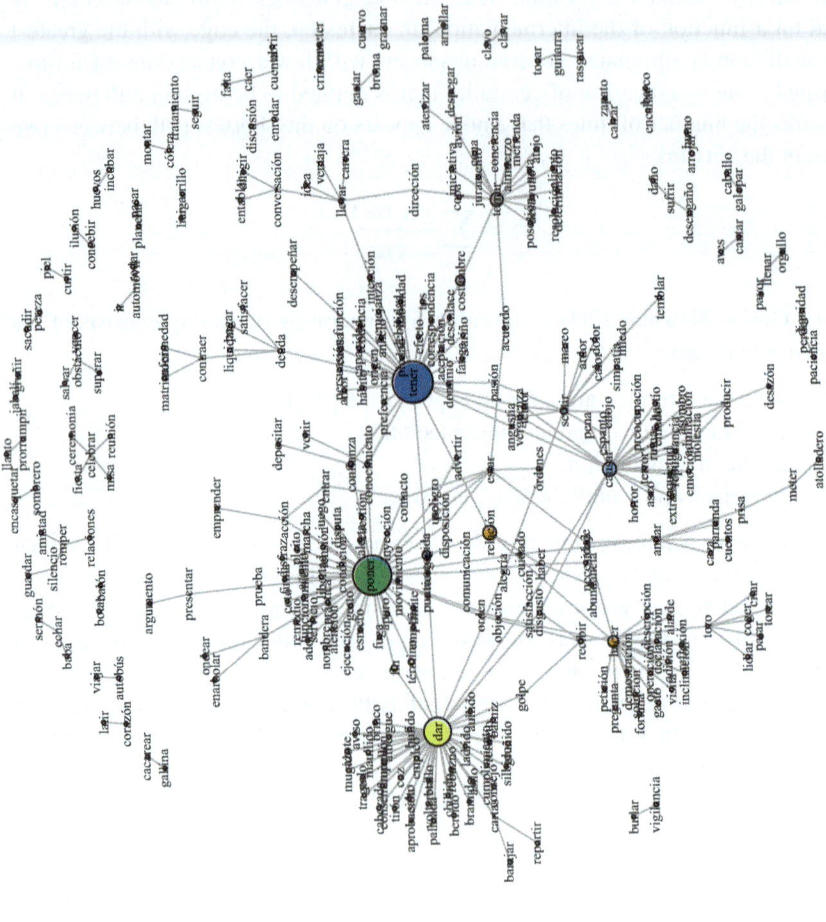

Fig. 3.2 Communities in the functional collocations graph

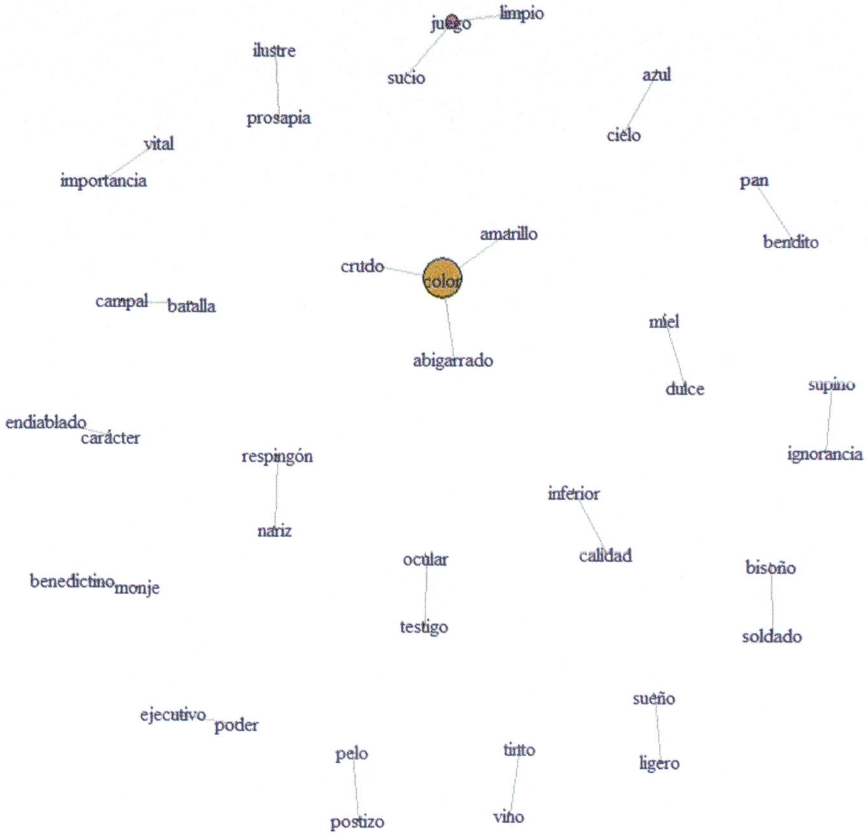

Fig. 3.3 Communities in the adjective + noun collected collocations graph

8 Conclusions

Techniques of collocation extraction based on association measures are useful, but their applicability to restricted collocations between a base and a collocate is limited. The work that we have developed takes advantage of the abundant amount of collocations in the general language dictionaries to enrich statistical rankings. Taking the Spanish dictionary DLVE as a reference, we have determined the definitions that constitute sources of functional collocations and lexical collocations. Given a set of words, we were interested in analyzing relationships of the following type: "recurrent combination," "used to define a," and "is in the contour of the definition of." Therefore, we have constructed a graph of word relationships, which constitutes a complex system to which network analysis techniques have been applied. The NoSQL graph databases give us a good alternative to the traditional relational databases to support this lexical resource. The design of the lexical database model has facilitated the use of network analysis tools that discriminate different categories of collocations, particularly functional and lexical collocations.

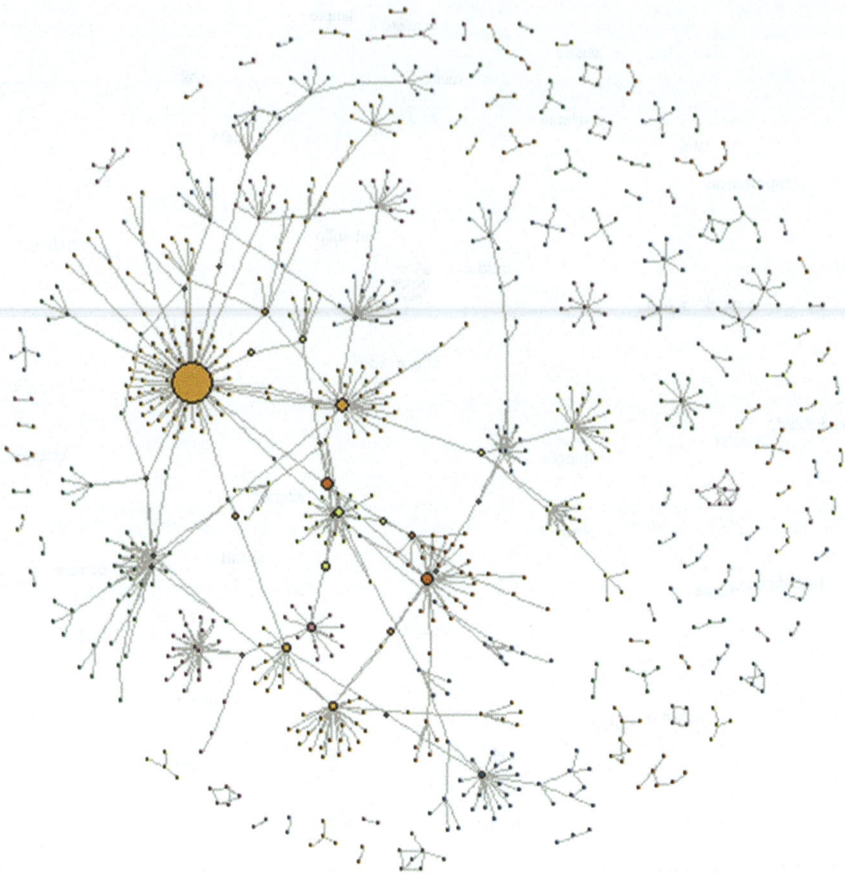

Fig. 3.4 Community structure for combinations in the corpus and in definitions

Bibliography

Alonso Ramos, M. (1994). Hacia una definición del concepto de colocación: De J. R. Firth a I. A. Mel'čuk. *Revista de Lexicografía, 1*, 9–28.

Alonso Ramos, M. (2002a). Colocaciones y contorno de la definición lexicográfica. *Lingüística Española Actual, 24*(1), 63–96.

Alonso Ramos, M. (2002b). *Diccionario de Colocaciones del Español*. http://www.dicesp.com/paginas. Accessed 20 October 2017.

Alonso, A., Millon, C., & Williams, G. (2011). Collocational networks and their application to an E-advanced Learner's dictionary of verbs in science (DicSci). In I. Kosem & K. Kosem (Eds.), *Electronic lexicography in the 21st century: New applications for new users: Proceedings of eLex 2011* (pp. 12–122). Liubliana: Trojina, Institute for Applied Slovene Studies.

Alvar Ezquerra, M. (1998). *Diccionario Ideológico de la Lengua Española*. Madrid: Vox.

Anthony, L. (2018). *AntConc (version 3.5.6) [computer software]*. Tokyo: Waseda University.

Baker, P. (2005). *Public discourses of gay men*. London: Routledge.

Baker, P. (2014). *Using corpora to analyse gender*. London: Bloomsbury.

Baker, P. (2016). The shapes of collocation. *International Journal of Corpus Linguistics, 21*(2), 139–164.
Bartsch, S. (2004). *Structural and functional properties of collocations in English. A corpus study of lexical and pragmatic constrains on lexical co-occurrence*. Tübingen: Gunter Narr Verlag.
Bosque, I. (2001). Sobre el concepto de colocación y sus límites. *Lingüística Española Actual, 23*(1), 9–40.
Bosque, I. (2004a). *REDES Diccionario combinatorio del español contemporáneo*. Madrid: Ediciones SM.
Bosque, I. (2004b). La direccionalidad en los diccionarios combinatorios y el problema de la selección léxica. In T. Cabré Monné (Ed.), *Lingüística teòrica: anàlisi i perspectives I* (pp. 13–58). Bellaterra: Universitat Autónoma de Barcelona (*Catalan Journal of Linguistics. Monografies; 2*).
Bosque, I. (2006). *Diccionario Combinatorio Práctico del Español Contemporáneo*. Madrid: SM.
Brezina, V., McEnery, T., & Wattam, S. (2015). Collocations in context: A new perspective on collocation networks. *International Journal of Corpus Linguistics, 20*(2), 139–173.
Cantos, P., & Sánchez, A. (2001). Lexical constellations: What collocates fail to tell. *International Journal of Corpus Linguistics, 6*(2), 199–228.
Castillo Carballo, M. (1997). El concepto de Unidad Fraseológica. *Revista de Lexicografía, IV*, 67–79.
Castillo Carballo, M. A. (1998). El término 'colocación' en la lingüística actual. *Lingüística Española Actual, 20*(1), 41–54.
Castillo Carballo, M. A. (2001). Colocaciones léxicas y variación lingüística: implicaciones didácticas. *Lingüística Española Actual, 23*(1), 133–143.
Church, K. W., & Hanks, P. (1990). Word association norms, mutual information, and lexicography. *Computational Linguistics, 16*(1), 22–29.
Corpas Pastor, G. (1996). *Manual de Fraseología española*. Madrid: Gredos.
Corpas Pastor, G. (2001). Apuntes para el estudio de la colocación. *Lingüística Española Actual, 23*(1), 41–56.
Corpas Pastor, G. (2003). *Diez años de investigación en fraseología: análisis sintáctico-semánticos, contrastivos y traductológicos*. Madrid: Iberoamericana.
Diccionario General de la Lengua Española. 2008. Barcelona: Vox.
Evert, S. (2005). *The statistics of word coocurrences. Word pairs and collocations*. (Unpublished PhD Thesis) Universität Stuttgart.
García Platero, J. M. (2002). Aspectos semánticos de las colocaciones. *Lingüística Española Actual, 24*(1), 25–34.
García Page, M. (2001). Adverbios restringidos y adverbios colocacionales. *Revista de lexicografía, 23*(1), 89–106.
Girvan, M., & Newman, M. E. (2002). Community structure in social and biological networks. *Proceedings of the National Academy of Sciences, 99*(12), 7821–7826.
Gries, S. T. (2013). John Benjamins Publishing Company. *International Journal of Corpus Linguistics, 18*(1), 137–165.
Hausmann, F. J. (1979). Un dictionnaire des collocations est-il possible? *Travaux de linguistique et de litterature, 17*(1), 187–195.
Hausmann, F. J., & Blumenthal, P. (2006). Présentation: collocation, corpus, dictionnaires. *Langue Française, 150*, 3–13.
Jackson, A. F., & Bolger, D. J. (2014). Using a high-dimensional graph of semantic space to model relationships among words. *Frontiers in Psychology, 5*, 385.
Jiménez Martínez, M. I. (2016). *Colocaciones y verbos soporte en latín: semántica y sintaxis del verbo pono*. (Unpublished PhD Thesis). Universidad Complutense de Madrid. http://eprints.ucm.es/44254/1/T39088.pdf. Accessed 24 March 2018.
Kolakzyc, E. D., & Csárdi, G. (2014). *Statistical analysis of network data with R* (Vol. 65). New York: Springer.
Koike, K. (1993). Caracterización y estructuras del verbo compuesto. *Hispanic, 37*, 14–29.
Koike, K. (2001). *Colocaciones léxicas en español actual*. Madrid: Universidad de Alcalá.

Leavitt, N. (2010). Will NoSQL databases live up to their promise? *Computer, 43*(2), 12–14.

McEnery, T. (2006). *Swearing in English: Bad language, purity and power from 1586 to the present*. Abington: Routledge.

Mel'čuk, I. (1998). Collocations and lexical functions. In A. P. Cowie (Ed.), *Phraseology. Theory, analysis and applications* (pp. 3–53). Oxford: Clarendon Press.

Molina-Plaza, S., and Sancho-Guinda, C. (2007). Collocational trends of de-lexicalised English verbs (have, make, take) and their Spanish homologues: A preliminary contrastive study. In Proceedins of the 26th international conference on Lexis and grammar, eds. C. Camugli, M. Constant and A. Dister. http://infolingu.univ-mlv.fr/Colloques/Bonifacio/proceedings/molina.pdf. Accessed 24 March 2018.

Penadés Martínez, I. (2001). ¿Colocaciones o locuciones verbales. *Lingüística Española Actual, 23*(1), 57–88.

Phillips, M. K. (1983). *Lexical macrostructure in science text* (Unpublished PhD Thesis). University of Birmingham, Birmingham, UK.

Phillips, M. (1985). *Aspects of text structure: An investigation of the lexical organisation of text*. Amsterdam: North-Holland.

Phillips, M. (1989). *Lexical Structure of Text*. Birmingham: ELR. In *University of Birmingham*.

Real Academia Española. (2017). *Diccionario de la Lengua Española*. Madrid: Espasa Calpe.

Robinson, I., Webber, J., & Eifrem, E. (2013). *Graph databases*. Sebastopol, CA: O'Reilly Media, Inc..

Santana, O., Pérez, J., Hernández, Z., Carreras, F., & Rodríguez, G. (1997). FLAVER: Flexionador y lematizador automático de formas verbales. *Lingüística Española Actual, 19*(2), 229–282.

Santana, O., Pérez, J., Carreras, F., Duque, J., Hernández, Z., & Rodríguez, G. (1999). FLANOM: Flexionador y lematizador automático de formas nominales. *Lingüística Española Actual, 21*(2), 253–297.

Santana-Suárez, S., Aguiar, J. R. P., Riudavets, F. J. C., Figueroa, Z. J. H., del Pino, J. C. R., Roca, M. D., & Rodríguez, G. R. (2007) Development of Support Services for Linguistic Research over the Internet TIN2004-03988.

Santana-Suárez, O., Pérez-Aguiar, J., Sánchez-Berriel, I., & Gutiérrez-Rodríguez, V. (2014). COLEXWEB, herramienta de consulta de las capacidades combinatorias de las palabras del español. *Lingüística Española Actual, 36*(2), 273–295.

Siepmann, D. (2005). Collocation, colligation and encoding dictionaries. Part I: Lexicological aspects. *International Journal of Lexicography, 18*(4), 409–443.

Scott, M. (2016). *WordSmith Tools version 7 [computer software]*. Stroud: Lexical analysis software.

Seco, M. (1978). Problemas formales de la definición. In J. L. García-Arias, M. V. Conde, & J. Martínez-Álvarez (Eds.), *Estudios ofrecidos a E. Alarcos Llorach* (Vol. II, pp. 217–239). Oviedo: Universidad.

Seco, M. (1979). El contorno de la definición. In G. Suárez-Blanco (Ed.), *Homenaje a Samuel Gili Gaya (in memoriam)* (pp. 189–191). Barcelona: Vox.

Seco, M., Ramos, G., & Andrés, O. (1992). *El diccionario del español actual*. Madrid: Aguilar.

Vincze, O., & Alonso Ramos, M. (2013). Incorporating frequency information in a collocation dictionary: Establishing a methodology. In C. Vargas (Ed.), *Corpus resources for descriptive and applied studies. Current challenges and future directions: Selected papers from the 5th international conference on Corpus linguistics (CILC2013)* (pp. 241–248). Amsterdam: Elsevier.

Vincze, O., Mosqueira, E., & Alonso Ramos, M. (2011). An online collocation dictionary of Spanish. In I. Boguslavsky & L. Wanner (Eds.), *Proceedings of the 5th international conference on meaning-text theory* (pp. 275–286). Barcelona: Árbol Académico.

Wanner, L., Ferraro, G., & Moreno, P. (2016). Towards distributional semantics-based classification of collocations for collocation dictionaries. *International Journal of Lexicography, 30*(2), 167–186.

Williams, G. (1998). Collocational networks: Interlocking patterns of lexis in a corpus of plant biology research articles. *International Journal of Corpus Linguistics, 3*(1), 151–171.

Williams, G., Decesaris, J., & Alonso, A. (2017). Studying lexical meaning in context: From collocation to collocational networks and resonance. In S. Torner & E. Bernal (Eds.), *Collocations and other lexical combinations in Spanish. Theoretical, lexicographical and applied perspectives* (pp. 41–72). London: Routledge.

Chapter 4
Collocation Graphs and Networks: Selected Applications

Vaclav Brezina

Abstract This chapter discusses the notion of collocation graphs and networks, which not only represent visualisation of the collocational relationship traditionally displayed in a tabular form but also constitute a novel analytical technique. This technique, although originally proposed by Philips in 1985, has only recently gained prominence with the introduction of the #LancsBox tool (Brezina et al., Int J Corpus Linguist 20:139–173, 2015), which can, among other things, build collocation graphs and networks on the fly. Simple collocation graphs and collocation networks show association and cross-association between words in language and discourse and can thus be used in a range of areas of linguistic and social research. This chapter demonstrates the use of the collocation network technique in (i) discourse analysis, (ii) language learning research and (iii) lexicography, providing three case studies that focus not only on the variety of applications but also on different methodological choices involved in using the technique.

1 Introduction

In essence, collocation is a phenomenon concerned with repeated co-occurrence of words in texts. There is something profoundly simple yet exceptionally insightful about the immediate space that words share with each other in texts. Investigating collocations thus creates an opportunity for looking into the fundamental fabric of text or speech through the lens of connection and association between words. Collocation is a broad phenomenon with fuzzy edges and multiple possible definitions (e.g. Gries 2013). In this chapter, I assume a simple Firthian notion of collocation as 'the habitual co-occurrence of words' (Firth 1957: 2), which is identified in corpora statistically using a range of association measures (Evert 2008, Gablasova et al. 2017b). Thus, from an analytical point of view, we employ corpus techniques (e.g.

V. Brezina (✉)
Lancaster University, Lancaster, UK
e-mail: v.brezina@lancaster.ac.uk

P. Cantos-Gómez, M. Almela-Sánchez (eds.), *Lexical Collocation Analysis*, Quantitative Methods in the Humanities and Social Sciences,
https://doi.org/10.1007/978-3-319-92582-0_4

Table 4.1 Collocates of 'love' in BE06 (CPN: 03 – MI(5), L3-R3, C: 5.0-NC: 5.0)

Collocate	MI-score	Freq. (coll.)	Freq. (corpus)
affair	8.86	5	37
fell	8.52	14	131
falling	8.52	5	47
fallen	8.37	5	52
me	5.57	23	1667
I'm	5.30	5	437
life	5.12	8	791

McEnery and Hardie 2011; Brezina and Gablasova 2018) to uncover patterns of frequent and/or exclusive co-occurrence of words and compare the strength of their association. For example, the first two words of this chapter (in 'essence') form a collocation, which on average occurs about four times per one million words (based on the British National Corpus); this is about a quarter of cases, in which the word 'essence' occurs but only 0.02 per cent of cases in which the frequent English preposition *in* occurs. This fact can be expressed statistically as Delta $P = 0.22$; 0.0002 (for more information about the Delta P association measure, see Gries 2013).

In addition to providing numerical information about the collocational relationship between two words, which has traditionally been displayed in a tabular form (e.g. Table 4.1 above), we can also draw a graph (e.g. Fig. 4.1), which represents a visual summary of the connections between words. Visualisation of collocation is a powerful interpretative technique suitable for the analysis of complex linguistic relationships in corpus data. As an example, the graph in Fig. 4.1 shows the words immediately preceding the node (word of interest) 'essence' in BE06[1], a one-million-word corpus of written English (Baker 2009). The length of the links (edges) in the graph shows the strength of the collocation, here measured by the simple frequency of co-occurrence: the closer the collocate is displayed to the node, the stronger the relationship (for more explanation see Sect. 2). Such a graph, which we call a simple collocation graph, can be expanded into a more complex collocation network. A collocation network is a graph that includes multiple nodes, their respective unique collocates, as well as shared links and shared collocates. Simple collocation graphs and collocation networks have a large potential not only to effectively summarise data but also, as I demonstrate in this chapter, to bring new insights into corpus linguistic analysis.

Traditionally, collocations were considered as discrete phenomena displayed as lists of collocates in a tabular form. Collocations, however, as I discuss in this chapter, can also be regarded as connected entities, which can be displayed in the form of collocation graphs and networks. While collocation graphs provide a useful visual display of the most important collocates around a node as an alternative to

[1]In this case, the asymmetrical collocation span 1 L 0R (one word to the left zero to the right) has been chosen to focus the attention to a particular grammatical frame.

Fig. 4.1 Collocation graph of 'essence' in BE06 (CPN (Collocation parameter notation (CPN) is used throughout this chapter to report settings used for collocation identification. See Sect. 2 for more details.): 01 – frequency (1), L1-R0, C: 1.0-NC: 1.0)

the traditional collocation table, collocation networks go one step further, indicating complex relationships between multiple words (nodes). Collocation networks thus show associations, cross-associations and shared as well as unique collocates – information about the use of words that is not readily available from the traditional form of display. The idea of collocation networks goes back to Phillips (e.g. Phillips 1985) and has been used in studies on terminology (Williams 1998), historical/social development of language (McEnery 2006) and online discourse (Brezina 2016). Until recently, however, producing collocation networks involved considerable manual labour. With the introduction of #LancsBox (Brezina et al. 2015), which automatically identifies collocations and builds collocation networks on the fly, this task has become much more manageable and accessible to researchers. An important note needs to be made at this stage. Although superficially similar to word maps in a thesaurus (e.g. Visual Thesaurus 2018), collocation networks are based on a very different principle. While the thesaurus provides information about the paradigmatic relationship (synonymy, hyponymy, etc.) between words, collocation networks are primarily oriented towards the syntagmatic relationship. They thus show the associations in discourse, not in a dictionary.

This chapter first discusses the concept of collocation graphs and collocation networks. After this, three mini case studies using #LancsBox are offered to demonstrate the use of collocation networks in three areas of language analysis: (i) discourse analysis, (ii) language learning and (iii) lexicography.

2 Collocation Graphs and Networks: Concept Exploration

A traditional form of presentation of the collocational relationship is a table with collocates ordered according to the decreasing strength of the association between the node and the collocates. For example, Table 4.1 shows top seven collocates in the L3 R3 span (three words to the left, three words to the right) of the node *love* (as a grapheme/type) in the BE06 corpus of current written British English (Baker 2009). The collocates are ranked according to their MI (mutual information) score value; MI score is a common association measure used in corpus linguistics (Gablasova et al. 2017b).

The same information can be displayed in a graphical format in the form of a collocation graph (Fig. 4.2). A collocation graph shows the relationship between the node and its collates as measured by a particular collocation statistic (association

Fig. 4.2 Collocation graph – free view: 'love' in BE06 (CPN: 03 – MI(5), L3-R3, C: 5.0-NC: 5.0)

measure). The length of the link (edge) between the node and the collocates is inversely proportional to the strength of association: the stronger the association, the shorter the link. As can be seen in Fig. 4.2, the collocates most strongly associated with 'love' according to the MI-score are *affair*, *fell*, *falling* and *fallen*. On the other hand, *me*, *I'm* and *life* are not that strongly associated. In addition, the graph also shows the frequency of the individual collocations (co-occurrences of node + collocate): a strong colour shows a more frequent co-occurrence. Thus, for example, in the outer circle, *me* and *life* are more frequent collocates than *I'm*.

In a symmetrical window such as 3L-3R, another collocation dimension that we can measure is the position of the collocate in the text. Some collocates occur in syntactic (linear) positions that precede the node, others in positions that follow. For example, different forms of the verb *to fall* always precede the node *love* to form the phrase *to fall in love*; on the other hand, *affair* always follows *love* to form the expression *love affair.* This form of display leads to an overlap (as in Fig. 4.3) if multiple collocates occur in the same linear position. Figure 4.3 also displays the prevalent tendency of individual collocates to appear mostly left or mostly right of the node which is established by calculating the proportion of cases which occur to the left/right out of all cases. For example, *life* typically follows the node *love* as in the example below:

(1) The BBC was clear that Mr Blunkett's *love life* was absolutely his own affair (BE06, B01).

Fig. 4.3 Collocation graph – positional view: 'love' in BE06 (CPN: 03 – MI(5), L3-R3, C: 5.0-NC: 5.0)

In some cases, however, *life* can precede *love* as in the example below:

(2) Do you believe in *life* after *love* (BE06, K)?

In Fig. 4.3, the collocate *life* is therefore displayed leaning to the right but not completely right of the node. *I'm* is a similar case to *life* in terms of its position around the node; note that the decision whether a collocate is displayed above or below the node is motivated purely by readability (ease of display) and does not relate to any properties of the collocate[2]. Apart from the two right-leaning collocates, the graph in Fig. 4.3 shows also the collocate *me*, which gravitates to the left with slight prevalence of examples such as (3) below.

(3) Dad needed to leave *me* to *love* the next child (BE06, K).

The position that is displayed in the graph helps us interpret the linguistic meaning of the collocation and provides a useful summary of the typical syntactic positions in which collocates occur.

So far, we have looked at only word forms (types) as the units of the collocational analysis. In Table 4.1 and Fig. 4.2, for instance, different inflectional forms of the verb *fall* appeared as three different collocates (*fallen*, *falling* and *fell*). For some types of analysis, it can be useful to work with lemmas as the units of analysis. For example, we can search for the lemma *love* as a verb, which will exclude all nominal uses of *love* but will include *loves*, *loving* and *loved* as inflectional forms of the verb *love*. Collocates are then identified as described above, this time looking for lemmas rather than types. The resulting graph can be seen in Fig. 4.4. Each collocate in the graph represents a headword (dictionary form) and its word class is indicated by a tag.

Finally, we need to consider an important feature of collocation, which is connectivity (Phillips 1985; Brezina et al. 2015). Collocations in language and discourse enter into a rich network of meaning associations and cross-associations. Displaying and analysing these networks help us uncover important relationships in language and discourse. Collocation connectivity cannot be easily and efficiently displayed in a tabular form; the best form of display of connected collocations is a complex collocation graph that we call a collocation network. Figure 4.5 shows a collocation network which highlights the connections between three words (types): *love*, *life* and *family*. We can see that *love* is connected with *family* indirectly via *life*. *Family* and *life* have, in addition, two shared collocates *whole* and *entire*: we talk about *whole life/family* and *entire life/family*. We can also explore collocates that are unique (not shared) to each of the three nodes. For further theoretical discussion of the concept of collocation networks and its use, see Phillips (1985), Brezina et al. (2015), Baker (2016) and Brezina (2016).

---

[2]This is a necessary concession when 'translating' the linear nature of texts and discourse into a graphical display. Users need to remember this as one of the conventions of displaying collocates operating in the 'Flatland' (Tufte 2006).

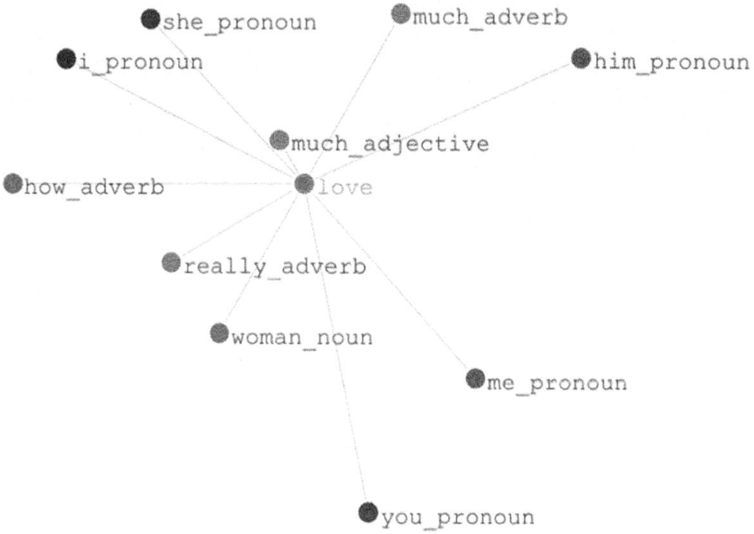

Fig. 4.4 Collocation graph – positional view, lemmatised: LOVE in BE06 (CPN: 03 – MI(5), L3-R3, C: 5.0-NC: 5.0)

Although collocation graphs and networks are identified and displayed automatically using #LancsBox (Brezina et al. 2015), the researcher needs to make a number of principled decisions about the parameters of collocations such as the choice of the association measure, threshold values, span, etc. These are discussed in more detail in Gablasova et al. (2017b). For standardised reporting of these values, Brezina et al. (2015) propose a system called collocation parameter notation (CPN) used also in this chapter. The pieces of information (parameters) that need to be reported are summarised in Table 4.2. These parameters include the statistic ID (referring to a list of statistical measures in Brezina et al. 2015), statistic name, statistic cut-off value, span, minimum collocate frequency, minimum collocation frequency and any additional filters applied. The suggested form of reporting is listed in the last row of Table 4.2.

In sum, the aspects of the collocational relationship that we can explore using the technique of collocation graphs and networks are: (i) strength, (ii) frequency, (iii) and 'position' together (iv) collocate unit and (v) connectivity. These features of the collocational relationships can be exploited in linguistic analysis as is shown in the case studies below.

3 Case Study 1: Collocation Networks in Discourse Analysis

This case study investigates the perception of 'East European immigrants' by analysing the associations with the words 'immigrant' and 'immigrants' in reader comments under articles in two British newspapers: *The Guardian* and

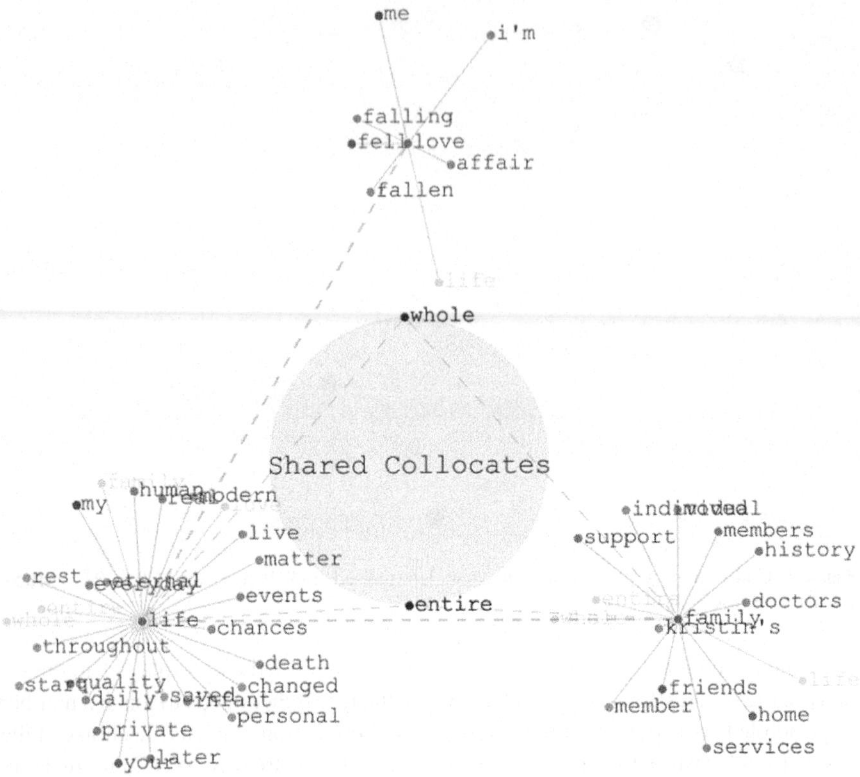

Fig. 4.5 Collocation network: 'love', 'life' and 'family' (CPN: 03 – MI(5), L3-R3, C: 5.0-NC: 5.0)

Table 4.2 Collocation parameter notation (Brezina et al. 2015: 146)

Statistic ID	Statistic name	Statistic cut-off value	L and R span	Minimum collocate freq. (C)	Minimum collocation freq. (NC)	Filter
4b	MI2	3	L5-R5	5	1	function words removed
4b-MI2(3), L5-R5, C5-NC1; function words removed						

the *Daily Mail*. These two newspapers attract a different type of reader. While *The Guardian*, which can be categorised as a serious 'heavy weight' paper politically leaning to the left, attracts readers whose values typically align with the newspaper's positions, the *Daily Mail*, a right-wing mass market newspaper, has a more general readership (McNair 2009). The comments express readers' opinions, perspectives and ideologies in response to a particular content of the newspaper articles. The focus of the analysis is the issue of immigration, a topic that has been widely researched using different methods, including the methods of corpus linguistics (e.g. Blinder and Allen 2016; KhosraviNik 2009; Gabrielatos and Baker 2008).

This study contributes to the debate by applying collocation network analysis to investigate the main associations with immigrants in the reader comment data. Before describing the methodology, a small historical remark contextualising the research is required: in January 2014, Britain opened its job market to citizens from Romania and Bulgaria. In the run up to this event, the British press frequently debated the possible impact of this decision on British economy and the quality of life in Britain. In the media, comparisons were also made with a previous event 10 years earlier (2004) when the job market opened to citizens of Poland, Hungary, the Czech Republic and Slovakia. Interestingly, after the 2016 Brexit referendum, which brought the decision for Britain to leave the European Union, the pre-Brexit debates about immigration can be seen as a contributing factor to the result of the referendum and thus of high social importance.

3.1 Method

The corpus used in this study is a small purpose-built sample of comments occurring under articles in *The Guardian* and *Daily Mail* newspapers. 'East/Eastern European(s)' was used as the search term to identify the relevant articles in the two newspapers in the period from 2010 to 2013. 'East(ern) Europeans' is a collective term frequently used by the British press to refer to people from new European Union countries (e.g. Romania, Bulgaria, the Czech Republic or Poland). Overall, 1,024,495 tokens were extracted from *The Guardian* (GU corpus) and 729,042 from the *Daily Mail* (DM corpus). Table 4.3 provides the details about the two corpora used.

As is apparent from Table 4.3, there are over ten thousand comments in each corpus with *The Guardian* readers providing slightly fewer but on average longer comments than the *Daily Mail* readers. The mean comment length was 101 tokens in the GU corpus and 55 tokens in the DM corpus; this means that an average reader comment in *The Guardian* was almost twice as long as an average comment in the *Daily Mail*. The search term used in the collocation analysis was the nominal lemma 'immigrant'. The logDice score was selected as the association measure to identify frequent and exclusive associations (Gablasova et al. 2017b; Brezina 2018). It is important to note that the topics, the views and the nature of the articles published in the two newspapers will have an effect on the types of reader comments left below the articles. What is analysed here, however, is not the relationship between

Table 4.3 Reader comment data

Corpora	Comments	Unique contributors	Tokens	Mean comment length (tokens)
GU corpus	10,193	4072	1,024,495	101
DM corpus	13,265	6093	729,042	55
TOTAL	23,458	10,165	1,753,537	75

the types of articles published in the two newspapers and the types of comments posted by the readers. The focus is solely on the discourse produced by the readers in reaction to articles which included the search term 'East/Eastern European(s)' in the given period.

3.2 Results and Discussion

Figures 4.6 and 4.7 display the results of the collocation analysis in the form of simple collocation graphs showing the collocates of the lemma 'immigrant' (subsuming the singular and plural forms) in the two corpora (GU and DM). In the broad analysis of the reader comments, we are interested in the main conceptual connections; Figs. 4.6 and 4.7 have therefore focused only on nouns, verbs and adjectives as collocates. Because the position of the collocates around the node is a useful indicator of the type of syntactic frames the node and the collocates occur in

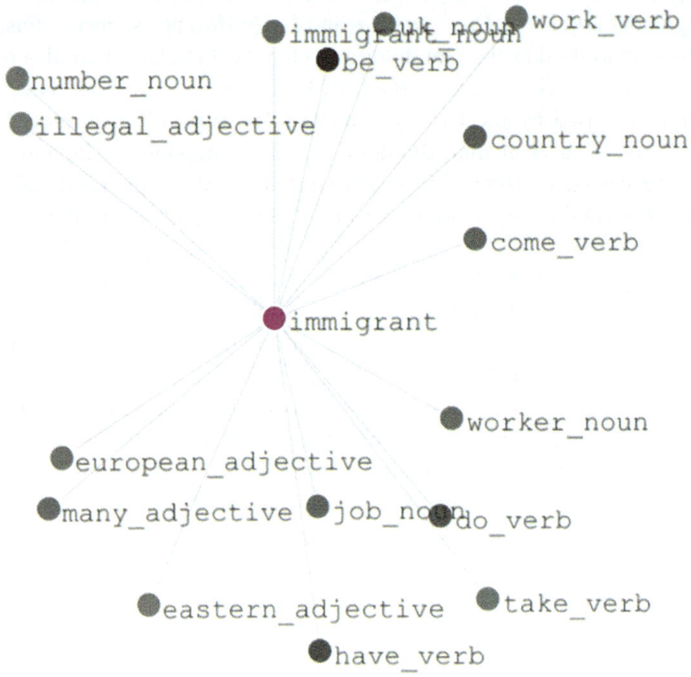

Fig. 4.6 Collocations around the lemma IMMIGRANT in GU (9a-logDice(9), R5-L5, C10-NC10; only nouns, verbs and adjectives shown (For a discussion on the motivation of different collocation settings, see Gablasova et al. (2017b))

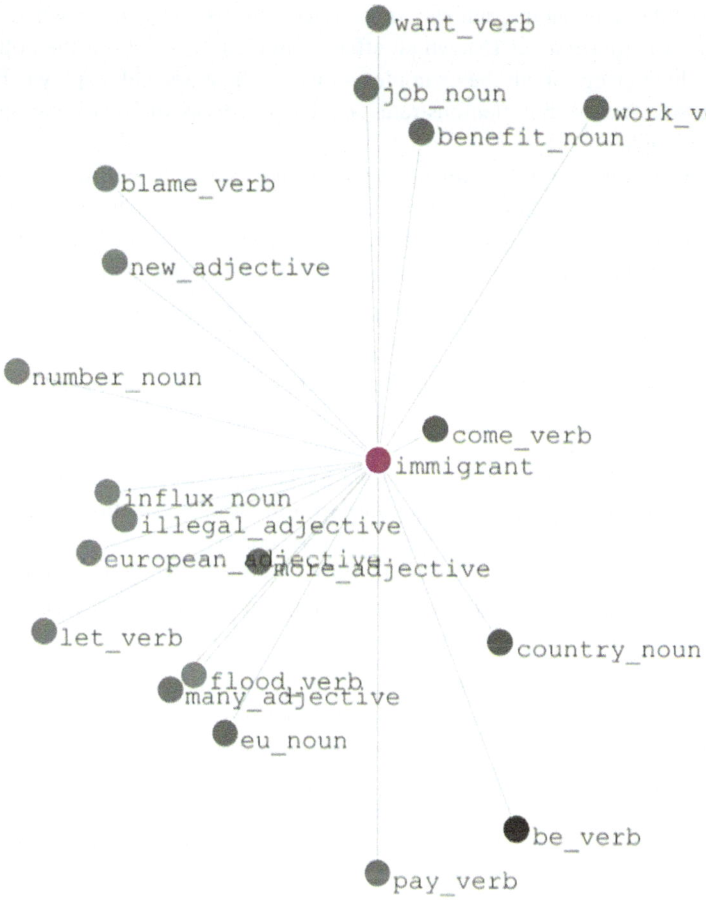

Fig. 4.7 Collocations around the lemma IMMIGRANT in DM (9a-logDice(9), R5-L5, C10-NC10; only nouns, verbs and adjectives shown)

(see Sect. 2), Figs. 4.6 and 4.7 offer the positional view, where collocates displayed left of the node (mostly) precede the node in text, while collocates displayed right of the node (mostly) follow it in text.

We can see that there is a comparable number of collocates in the two graphs: 16 in the GU corpus and 19 in the DM corpus. Out of these, nine collocates are shared by the two corpora: *be_verb*, *come_verb*, *country_noun*, *european_adjective*, *illegal_adjective*, *job_noun*, *many_adjective*, *number_noun*, and *work_verb*. This, however, does not mean that these collocates are used in the same contexts in both corpora. The collocation graphs (same as collocation tables) need always be interpreted with the help of other corpus linguistic techniques such as concordances. While collocation graphs represent an abstraction based on multiple examples of word co-occurrence, these abstractions need to be interpreted referring back to the examples and their contexts. In practice, this is made easy when using #LancsBox (Brezina et al. 2015), which offers a simple right-click-on-the-collocate function, which brings up all the examples on which the graphical display is based. The discussion below thus demonstrates a typical process of interpretation of a collocation graph.

Returning to our example with immigration, the concordance lines show that the adjective *illegal* is employed predominantly in negative contexts in the DM comments (see examples 4 and 5 below), while the GU corpus includes a number of instances where the descriptor *illegal* is challenged (examples 6 and 7).

(4) Must come OUT of the EU NOW and send home all *illegal immigrants* NOW I am sick to death of reading articles like this (DM corpus).
(5) I won't even get into the *ILLEGAL immigrants* and how easy we have made it for them (DM corpus).
(6) Rarely is the distinction made between asylum seekers, immigrants and *illegal immigrants*. Personally, I have no time for people who easily take a swipe at hard-working low-paid legal migrants who often take jobs that unemployed UK citizens sometimes find unpalatable (GU corpus).
(24) Also irritating when the *Daily Mail*/BNP crowd posting here repeatedly confuse *'illegal' immigrants* with EU citizens, who have every right to be in Britain (GU corpus).

Focusing now on the unique collocates in the two corpora, the GU corpus includes many contextual and neutral collocates such as *do_verb*, *eastern_adjective*, *have_verb*, *immigrant_noun* and *uk_noun.* These collocates show that the debate revolves around immigrants from Eastern Europe to the UK, which is a mere reflection of the sampling of the corpus. The verbs *do* and *have* occur with a broad range of functions such as auxiliaries, lexical verbs with *immigrant(s)* as syntactic subjects and lexical verbs with *immigrant(s)* as syntactic objects in the GU reader discourse; these therefore (as is clear from the concordance lines behind the graphical display) do not point to any specific topic of a discussion about immigrants.

There are only two unique collocates in the GU corpus that highlight a particular topic of or a strand in the debate: *take_verb* and *worker_noun.* This is connected with question of whether immigrant workers take jobs of UK workers in the competitive job market. Examples of this debate can be seen below:

(8) What some 'working-class' Brits fail to understand is that non-British workers (both *immigrants* and Eastern European *workers*, again, different categories) put a lot more into the British welfare state than get out of (GU corpus).
(9) His wife may not need to work because of the high value of the cash that the *immigrant worker* can send home, so relatively fixed costs like childcare and mortgages become irrelevant (GU corpus).
(10) Brown says British jobs for British people, then we get the results in. *Immigrants take* 81% of new jobs (GU corpus).

Finally, let us look at the unique collocates in the DM corpus. These *are benefit_noun*, *blame_verb*, *eu_noun*, *flood_verb*, *influx_noun*, *let_verb*, *more_adjective*, *new_adjective*, *pay_verb*, and *want_verb*. They can be categorised into three main groups: (i) contextual (*eu_noun*), (ii) descriptive/evaluative (*flood_verb*, *influx_noun*, *more_adjective*, *new_adjective*, *benefit_noun*) and (iii) action-oriented (*blame_verb*, *pay_verb*, *want_verb*, *let_verb*). The only contextual or context-setting collocate is *eu* positioning the debate around immigration from the EU. The descriptive/evaluative collocates show the main narrative of the debate: there are a large number of new immigrants already in the UK or soon coming to the UK claiming benefits, etc. The negatively evaluative terms such as *flood* or *influx* are used to express the metaphorical connection between immigration and a natural disaster (see examples 11–12).

(11) Jobs, *benefits* and housing will all be given to a massive *influx* of *immigrants* (DM corpus).
(12) It's no surprise that we are in this state; labour desperately wanted a *flood* of *immigrants* into the country (DM corpus).

The last group of collocates is action-oriented collocates in a broad sense because all of them are verbs. These occur in a range of contexts, and as can be seen from the syntactic positions displayed in the graph in Fig. 4.7, *immigrants* are sometimes syntactic subjects, other times syntactic object in the constructions. The examples of this aspect of the debate include the following:

(13) Don't *blame* the *immigrants*; they are just after a better quality of life (DM corpus).
(14) Wait only when the country is completely over run will they learn, because the *immigrants* won't be *paying* any tax to fund the madness (DM corpus).
(15) Should I *pay* council tax to fund *immigrants* to ruin our country (DM corpus)?
(16) We don't *want* or need anymore *immigrants* (DM corpus).
(17) Don't *let immigrants* in to the country (DM corpus).

4 Case Study 2: Collocation Networks in Language Learning of *Make*, *Take* and *Do*

Our ability to communicate fluently in real time depends to a large extent on the phraseological competence, that is, the ability to store, access and produce prefabricated chunks of language such as multi-word expressions (*would like to*) or lexico-grammatical frames (*as far as X is concerned*). This competence represents a key aspect in communicating in a native-like, effortless and error-free manner. As a result, phraseological competence has occupied a prominent role in research on language learning/use by L1 and L2 users for decades (e.g. Paquot 2017; Howarth 1998). However, despite the attention given to the topic so far, significant gaps still remain in our understanding of the mechanisms of phraseological competence development. In addition, most of our knowledge of phraseological competence is based on written data; spoken (unedited) production of L2 users has rarely been studied from the developmental perspective on phraseology. For references on spoken L2 production, see, e.g. Aijmer 2011; for references on L2 phraseology, see, e.g. Stefanowitsch and Gries 2003 and Paquot and Granger 2012.

This study aims to address this gap by investigating phraseology in spoken L2 English. It uses the technique of collocation graphs to investigate the development of phraseological competence at three proficiency levels B1, B2 and C1/C2 of the Common European Framework of Reference (Council of Europe 2001).

4.1 Method

This study is based on the Trinity Lancaster Corpus (TLC) of spoken L2 English (Gablasova et al. 2017c), which provides a unique insight into learner speech. The corpus samples speakers with different L1 s (first languages) including Spanish, Italian, Hindi and Chinese. Three subcorpora of semi-formal speech based on the conversation and discussion tasks in the TLC were used to trace the development of phraseological complexity of combinations that include three frequent English verbs: *make*, *take* and *do*. The subcorpora represented three different proficiency bands from B1 to C2. Table 4.4 provides an overview of the dataset.

As can be seen from Table 4.4, the proficiency-based subcorpora differ in terms of the token count and the number of speakers included. The largest difference is between the advanced subcorpus and the other two subcorpora. This presents a methodological challenge if we want to directly compare collocations based on these subcorpora because smaller corpora overall include less evidence about collocation than larger ones. In order for the collocation analysis to be comparable across the three subcorpora, a relative frequency cut-off point was chosen instead of a typical absolute frequency cut-off point. The relative frequency was calculated in relation to the frequency of the node (see Table 4.5). The relative frequency was thus not calculated per, e.g. 10,000 or one million words, as is usual in corpus linguistics, but in reference to the frequency of the node in the subcorpora because the possible frequency of a collocate is directly related to the node frequency, not the overall size of the subcorpus. For example, *make* occurs 306 times in the advanced subcorpus. If we stipulate that a minimum acceptable frequency of the collocation in this corpus is 4, we can calculate that the minimum required frequency in the intermediate subcorpus is 6 because the frequency of the node (*make*) is approximately 1.5 times

Table 4.4 Three proficiency-based TLC subcorpora used in the research

	Pre-intermediate (B1)	Intermediate (B2)	Advanced (C1/C2)
Speakers	266	252	143
Tokens	220,333	262,307	170,935
Types	10,595	12,316	8,784
Lemmas	10,360	11,787	8,325

Table 4.5 Frequency of *make*, *take* and *do* and relative cut-off point values

	Pre-intermediate (B1)		Intermediate (B2)		Advanced (C1/C2)	
Verb lemmas (nodes)	Freq.	Cut-off	Freq.	Cut-off	Freq.	Cut-off
make	388	5	438	6	306	4
take	380	5	354	4	337	4
do	1,353	5	1,386	5	1,178	4

greater in the intermediate subcorpus than in the advanced subcorpus. All cut-off point frequencies for this analysis are listed in Table 4.5.

The MI score was selected as the association measure, which highlights exclusive and rare combinations of words (Gablasova et al. 2017b). For the purposes of this study, the MI score was ideally suited to highlight phraseological units emerging in the developmental process; the MI-score was used together with the frequency cut-off points from Table 4.5 to ensure that there is enough evidence in the corpus for the collocation. The searches were for lemmas (all inflected forms combined) of the verbs *make*, *take* and *do*. The collocates are displayed as types with inflected form not subsumed. This is because in this type of analysis, inflectional morphology can help distinguish between patterns such as:

(18) Make, *made*, etc. + *friends*
I *made friends* with grade three oh three year olds grade three (TLC, 7_SL_12).

(19) Make, made, etc. + fool of + friend
Friends who *make* a fool of their *friend* and if the friend does something wrong (TLC, 8_SL_7).

4.2 Results and Discussion

Figure 4.8 displays the results of the collocation analysis. With respect to the number of collocates, only *make* shows a clear tendency of an increase in the number of collocates across the proficiency bands; otherwise, there does not seem to be a clear relationship between increasing proficiency and a higher number of collocates. However, we can observe other proficiency-related patterns in the data. These are connected to the semantic properties of the collocations. First, with increasing proficiency, there is an increase in collocations whose constituent words (node + collocate) form a semantic unit. For example, *make* combines with *aware*, *easier*, *sure*, etc., which can be paraphrased using single lexical units such as *inform*, *facilitate* and *ensure*. Second, with increasing proficiency, the semantic units also become more abstract. For example, while at the B1 level the speakers produce combinations such as *take* + *bus* and *take* + *photos*, at higher proficiency levels, the combinations include *take* + *time* and *take* + *advantage*. The combinations with the verb *do* include both the uses of *do* as a lexical verb and as an auxiliary; only lexical verb combinations form semantic units such as *do* + *homework*, *exercise* and *research*.

In sum, the method of graphical display of collocates provided an access to different developmental patterns in the language learning process. A single figure (Fig. 4.8) can thus display the use of multiple items across multiple levels (in this case three verbs across three proficiency levels), allowing easy interpretation of the data and comparison between multiple analyses at once.

5 Case Study 3: Collocation Networks in Lexicography

Corpora have been widely used for lexicographic purposes (Granger and Paquot 2012). In addition to the analysis of concordances, lexicographers have increasingly used collocations to capture meaning patterns of a word. Indeed, one of the leading tools in electronic lexicography, Sketch Engine (Kilgarriff et al. 2014), implements word sketches, i.e. collocations of a word of interest categorised according to their syntactic position. A typical dictionary entry includes a definition of a word (Hanks 2016) and some related information (e.g. pronunciation, morphology, etymology, examples of use, etc.). As has been pointed out (Béjoint 2016:21), dictionaries for a general user rarely include words semantically related to the entry; if included, these are often limited to basic semantic relations such as synonymy or antonymy, hyponymy and meronymy (Murphy 2016). Going beyond these relations, we can see that words in language and discourse are connected via a rich network of conceptual links (Cope et al. 2011). In a classical book, Lakoff and Johnson (1980) introduce the idea of conceptual metaphors, metaphors inherent in our thinking and structuring of ideas:

> The most important claim we have made so far is that metaphor is not just a matter of language, that is, of mere words. We shall argue that, on the contrary, human thought processes are largely metaphorical. (Lakoff and Johnson 1980: 6)

The issue then arises how to find empirical evidence about these conceptual metaphors. Lakoff and Johnson (1980) list invented examples that point to similar conceptual structure between concepts connected through metaphors such as LOVE and JOURNEY, TIME and MONEY and ARGUMENT and WAR. The question which this study addresses is whether we can find empirical evidence about conceptual metaphor in corpus data using collocation networks. If so, collocation networks could help us in lexicographic description of words beyond the usual parameters observed in electronic lexicography.

5.1 Method (Lemmatised Collocation Network)

This case study uses BE06, a one-million-word corpus of written British English (Baker 2009). BE06 represents 15 major genres/registers of written English, ranging

Fig. 4.8 Collocation graphs of *make*, *take* and *do* for pre-intermediate, intermediate and advanced subcorpora (MI (3), L0-R3, NC: relative)

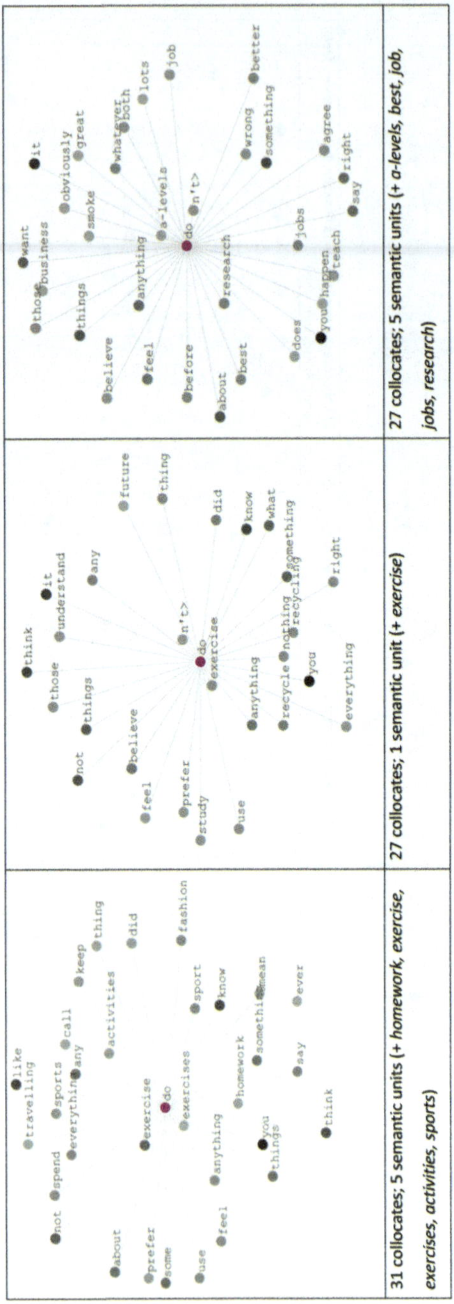

Fig. 4.8 (continued)

from newspaper language to general prose, academic writing and fiction. Each text in the corpus is a 2000-word sample from the given genre/register.

For demonstration purposes, three metaphors were chosen based on the Lakoff and Johnson (1980) list:

TIME is MONEY
LOVE is A JOURNEY
ARGUMENT is WAR

Collocation networks were built around the key conceptual words to explore the conceptual network of these key words. Each word was searched for as a nominal lemma (to include forms related by inflectional morphology); MI-score was used as the association measure with a cut-off point 5 for the statistic and 2 for the collocation frequency.

5.2 *Results and Discussion*

Figures 4.9, 4.10 and 4.11 display the results of the analysis. In each vertical panel, we can see collocates around the key conceptual words (in the top and at the bottom); in the middle, collocates shared by the two key words are highlighted. In this case, the focus of the analysis is not on unique collocates around each node (which largely unreadable) but on the collocates shared by the two key words through which these nodes are connected. Overall, we can see that all of the lemma pairs share mutual collocates, with TIME and MONEY (Fig. 4.9) having the largest number of shared collocates (13). Each pair ARGUMENT and WAR (Fig. 4.10) as well as LOVE and JOURNEY (Fig. 4.11) share four collocates. This is also related to the overall number of collocates that appear around each node with TIME and MONEY having both the largest number of shared and the largest number of unique collocates. For full comparability (which was not the aim in this study), a relative cut-off point for the collocate frequency would have to be used (see Sect. 4.1).

TIME and MONEY, with the richest network of shared collocates, demonstrate that both concepts can be quantified (*lot*, *amount*) and also prominently occur with verbs such as *have*, *save*, *spend* and *waste*. In addition, shared collocates such as *effort*, *worried* and *eventually* complement the picture. The concordance lines revealed that most frequent are the connections via the verbs. These uses of shared collocates are demonstrated in the examples below:

(20) You'll be *spending* a significant amount of *time* together on the day and . . . (BE06, E)
(21) FOREIGN AID- time to *spend* our *money* on our own people! (BE06, F)
(22) . . . in the race and *save* wasted *time* veering off-course. (BE06, E)
(23) Regardless of how much *time*, *effort*, or *money* you've *spent* building an iPhone application, Apple . . . (BE06, E)

The connections between ARGUMENT and WAR and LOVE and JOURNEY are not demonstrated as directly as the connection between TIME and MONEY.

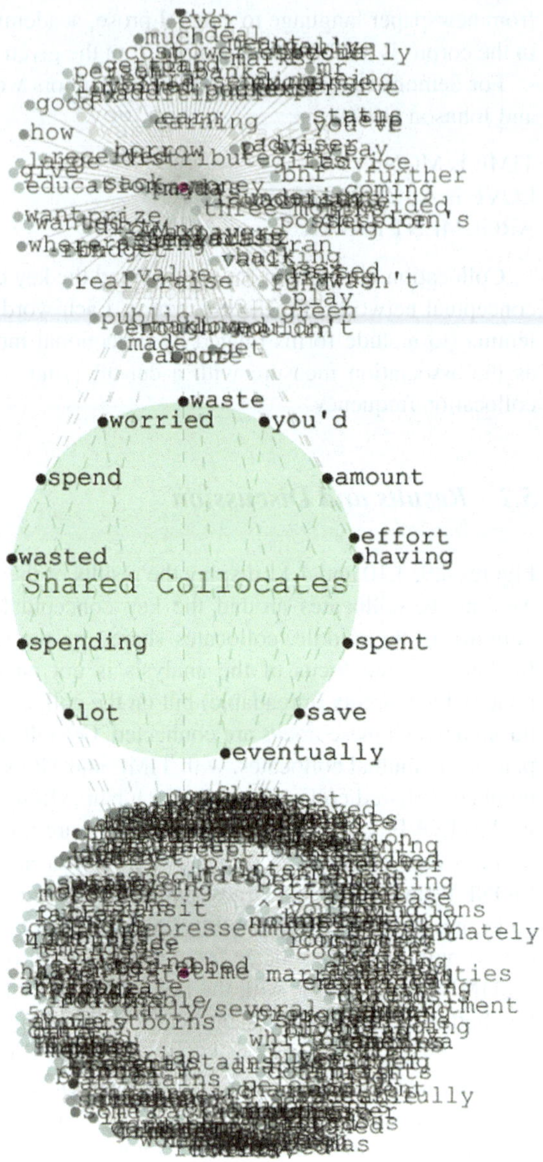

Fig. 4.9 Conceptual metaphor: TIME IS MONEY MI (5), L3-R3, C: 2, NC: 2)

This is because the conceptual spheres of WAR and ARGUMENT and LOVE and JOURNEY potentially include a variety of other key nodes beyond the two basic nodes searched for in each collocation graph. What we, however, can observe in Fig. 4.9 are fairly revealing connections, which may remain hidden without robust corpus data. For example, the following can be seen through the investigation of the concordance lines:

The preposition *against* combines with both WAR and ARGUMENT as in:

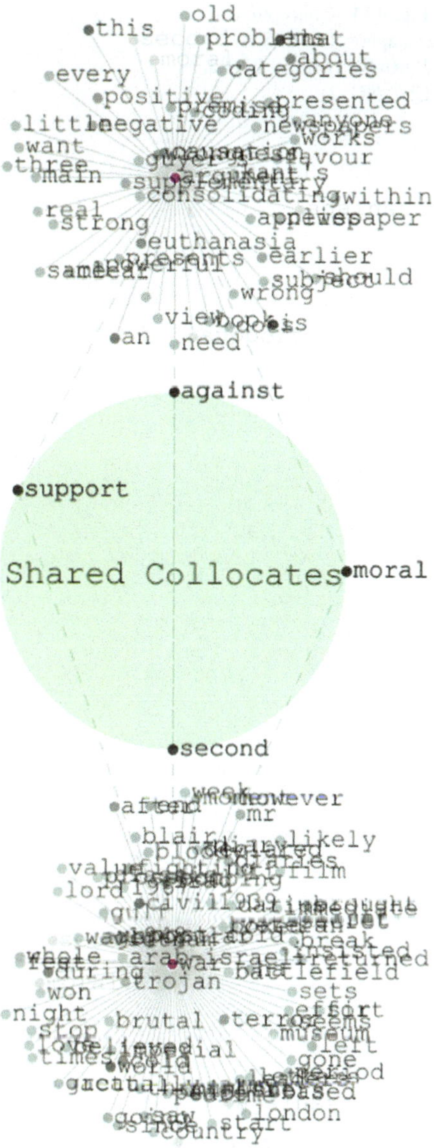

Fig. 4.10 Conceptual metaphor: ARGUMENT IS WAR MI (5), L3-R3, C: 2, NC: 2)

(24) . . . was of crucial value in the *war against* terrorism that had been fought . . . (BE06, N)

(25) . . . and presents a reduction ad absurdum *argument against* Kant's aesthetic system, which can be . . . (BE06, G)

This shared collocate frames them as events/processes that are defined through an opposition.

Fig. 4.11 Conceptual metaphor: LIVE IS A JORNEY (MI (5), L3-R3, C: 2, NC: 2)

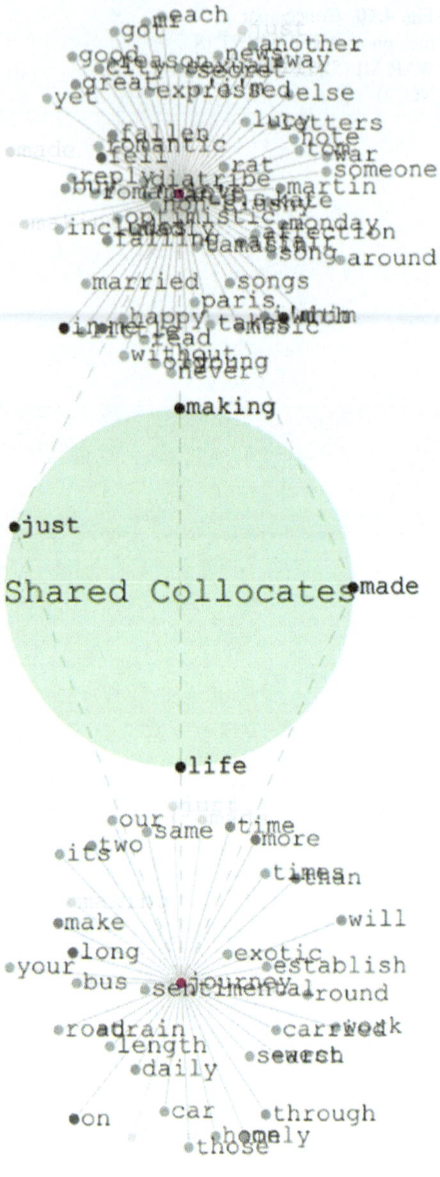

The verb *make* combines with both LOVE and JOURNEY as in:

(26) They are *making* the long *journey* from Cardiff. (BE06, B)
(27) Would I need to rehearse before *making love* to you? (BE06, G)

Overall, we can conclude that corpora provide clear evidence about conceptual metaphors in everyday language use. Collocation networks automatically identify the overlaps between collocates in multiple nodes (shared collocates). Although these would be available also when comparing individual collocation tables, the easy with which collocation networks display relationships between words makes collocation networks an ideal lexicographic tool. However, more work is required to translate these patterns into format suitable for dictionary entries.

6 Collocation Networks: Looking into the Future

When Phillips (1985) first defined the notion of collocation networks, he was primarily concerned with the investigation of 'aboutness' of single texts or very small corpora through collocation networks. More than 30 years later with the advances in technology, which allow us to efficiently process large amounts of linguistic data, the insights that collocation networks provide can go far beyond Phillips's (1985) original intention. This study demonstrated some possible uses of the collocation network technique to capture linguistic and conceptual connections in language and discourse.

As was shown, the collocation network technique is used in combination with other interpretative techniques such as concordancing to contextualise the findings displayed in the form of collocation graphs and networks. It also needs to be noted that collocation graphs and networks are only one of the possible ways of exploring collocations. For example, the traditional tabular form (which in #LancsBox is displayed next to the collocation graph) can in certain situations provide a more precise information (e.g. individual values of the association measure) than a collocation graph. On the other hand, a collocation graph or a collocation network can be a more powerful form of a summary than a table because it indicates through different features of the visual display (length of edges, shade of colour, position in graph, etc.) the main properties of the relationship between the node and its collocates; collocation networks, in addition, provide easy access to the information about shared collocates, which point to associations and cross-associations between words.

It is important to remember that connectivity between words in language is not an object of enquiry as such but an assumed starting point. Through statistical analysis of language, we highlight (and also downplay) different types of connections that align with our research questions (Gablasova et al. 2017a, b). For this reason, #LancsBox offers a range of statistical options for collocation extraction (Brezina et al. 2015), which allow us to zoom in onto the aspects of word co-occurrence we are interested in. The collocation network technique harbours a great potential to explore different linguistic, psychological and social topics that go beyond what was possible to demonstrate in this contribution. Future research using collocation networks should also include interdisciplinary studies combining corpus (observational) and experimental techniques and triangulating the obtained results (e.g. Baker and Egbert 2016). We could (and should) be asking questions about the extent to which the observed linguistic patterns (collocation graphs and networks) correlate with the way speakers process language and also about the extent these align with the beliefs and values of different groups of language users.

Acknowledgements I would like to thank the two anonymous reviewers for their helpful comments. The work on the chapter was supported by ESRC grants no. EP/P001559/1 and ES/K002155/1.

References

Aijmer, K. (2011). Well I'm not sure I think... the use of well by non-native speakers. *International Journal of Corpus Linguistics, 16*(2), 231–254.

Baker, P. (2009). The BE06 Corpus of British English and recent language change. *International Journal of Corpus Linguistics, 14*(3), 312–337.

Baker, P. (2016). The shapes of collocation. *International Journal of Corpus Linguistics, 21*(2), 139–164.

Baker, P., & Egbert, J. (Eds.). (2016). *Triangulating methodological approaches in corpus linguistic research*. New York: Routledge.

Béjoint, H. (2016). Dictionaries for general users: History and development; current issues. In P. Durkin (Ed.), *The Oxford handbook of lexicography* (pp. 7–24). Oxford: Oxford University Press.

Blinder, S., & Allen, W. L. (2016). Constructing immigrants: Portrayals of migrant groups in British national newspapers, 2010–2012. *International Migration Review, 50*(1), 3–40.

Brezina, V. (2016). Collocation networks. In P. Baker & J. Egbert (Eds.), *Triangulating methodological approaches in corpus linguistic research* (pp. 90–107). New York: Routledge.

Brezina, V. (2018). *Statistics for corpus linguistics: A practical guide*. Cambridge: Cambridge University Press.

Brezina, V., & Gablasova, D. (2018). The corpus method. In J. Culpeper, P. Kerswill, R. Wodak, T. McEnery, & F. Katamba (Eds.), *English language: Description, variation and context* (2nd ed.). Basingstoke: Palgrave Macmillan.

Brezina, V., McEnery, T., & Wattam, S. (2015). Collocations in context: A new perspective on collocation networks. *International Journal of Corpus Linguistics, 20*(2), 139–173.

Cope, B., Kalantzis, M., & Magee, L. (2011). *Towards a semantic web: Connecting knowledge in academic research*. Oxford: Chandos.

Council of Europe. (2001). *Common European framework of reference for languages: Learning, teaching, assessment*. Cambridge: Cambridge University Press.

Evert, S. (2008). Corpora and collocations. *Corpus linguistics. An international handbook, 2*, 1212–1248.

Firth, J. (1957). *Papers in linguistics*. Oxford: Oxford University Press.

Gablasova, D., Brezina, V., & McEnery, T. (2017a). Exploring learner language through corpora: Comparing and interpreting corpus frequency information. *Language Learning, 67*(S1), 155–179.

Gablasova, D., Brezina, V., & McEnery, T. (2017b). Collocations in corpus-based language learning research: Identifying, comparing and interpreting the evidence. *Language Learning, 67*(S1), 130–154.

Gablasova, D., Brezina, V., Mcenery, T., & Boyd, E. (2017c). Epistemic stance in spoken L2 English: The effect of task and speaker style. *Applied Linguistics, 38*(5), 613–637.

Gabrielatos, C., & Baker, P. (2008). Fleeing, sneaking, flooding: A corpus analysis of discursive constructions of refugees and asylum seekers in the UK press, 1996-2005. *Journal of English linguistics, 36*(1), 5–38.

Granger, S., & Paquot, M. (Eds.). (2012). *Electronic lexicography*. Oxford: OUP.

Gries, S. T. (2013). 50-something years of work on collocations. *International Journal of Corpus Linguistics, 18*(1), 137–166.

Hanks, P. (2016). Definition. In P. Durkin (Ed.), *The Oxford handbook of lexicography* (pp. 94–122). Oxford: Oxford University Press.

Howarth, P. (1998). Phraseology and second language proficiency. *Applied linguistics, 19*(1), 24–44.

KhosraviNik, M. (2009). The representation of refugees, asylum seekers and immigrants in British newspapers during the Balkan conflict (1999) and the British general election (2005). *Discourse & Society, 20*(4), 477–498.

Kilgarriff, A., Baisa, V., Bušta, J., Jakubíček, M., Kovář, V., Michelfeit, J., et al. (2014). The sketch engine: Ten years on. *Lexicography, 1*(1), 7–36.

Lakoff, G., & Johnson, M. (1980). *Metaphors we live by*. Chicago: University of Chicago Press.

McEnery, T. (2006). *Swearing in English: Bad language, purity and power from 1586 to the present*. London: Routledge.

McEnery, T., & Hardie, A. (2011). *Corpus linguistics: Method, theory and practice*. Cambridge: Cambridge University Press.

McNair, B. (2009). *News and journalism in the UK*. London: Routledge.

Murphy, L. M. (2016). Meaning relations in dictionaries: Hyponymy, meronymy, synonymy, antonymy, and contrast. In P. Durkin (Ed.), *The Oxford handbook of lexicography* (pp. 94–122). Oxford: Oxford University Press.

Paquot, M. (2017). The phraseological dimension in interlanguage complexity research. *Second Language Research*, 0267658317694221.

Paquot, M., & Granger, S. (2012). Formulaic language in learner corpora. *Annual Review of Applied Linguistics, 32*, 130–149.

Phillips, M. (1985). *Aspects of text structure: An investigation of the lexical organisation of text*. Amsterdam: North-Holland.

Stefanowitsch, A., & Gries, S. T. (2003). Collostructions: Investigating the interaction of words and constructions. *International Journal of Corpus Linguistics, 8*(2), 209–243.

Tufte, E. R. (2006). *Beautiful evidence*. Cheshire: Graphics Press.

Visual Thesaurus (2018). ThinkMap Inc. https://www.visualthesaurus.com/ [accessed 31/03/2018].

Williams, G. (1998). Collocational networks: Interlocking patterns of lexis in a corpusof plant biology research articles. *International Journal of Corpus Linguistics, 3*(1), 151–171.

Chapter 5
Multi-word Expressions: A Novel Computational Approach to Their Bottom-Up Statistical Extraction

Alexander Wahl and Stefan Th. Gries

Abstract In this paper, we introduce and validate a new bottom-up approach to the identification/extraction of multi-word expressions in corpora. This approach, called Multi-word Expressions from the Recursive Grouping of Elements (MERGE), is based on the successive combination of bigrams to form word sequences of various lengths. The selection of bigrams to be "merged" is based on the use of a lexical association measure, log likelihood (Dunning, *Computational Linguistics* 19:61–74, 1993). We apply the algorithm to two corpora and test its performance both on its own merits and against a competing algorithm from the literature, the adjusted frequency list (O'Donnell, *ICAME Journal* 35:135–169, 2011). Performance of the algorithms is evaluated via human ratings of the multi-word expression candidates that they generate. Ultimately, MERGE is shown to offer a very competitive approach to MWE extraction.

1 Introduction

Consider the following word sequences:

(1) a. Kick the bucket (idiom)
  b. Apple pie (compound)
  c. Strong coffee (habitual collocation, cf. *powerful coffee* is less correct)
  d. To put up with (multi-word verbs)
  e. You know what I mean? (speech formula)

A. Wahl
Radboud University, Donders Institute for Brain, Cognition and Behaviour, Nijmegen, Netherlands

S. T. Gries (✉)
University of California, Santa Barbara, Santa Barbara, CA

Justus Liebig University Giessen, Giessen, Germany
e-mail: stgries@linguistics.ucsb.edu

P. Cantos-Gómez, M. Almela-Sánchez (eds.), *Lexical Collocation Analysis*, Quantitative Methods in the Humanities and Social Sciences,
https://doi.org/10.1007/978-3-319-92582-0_5

f. A penny saved is a penny earned (proverb)
g. Barack Obama (proper name)[1]

While these sequences represent a variety of syntactic structures and lexical phenomena, they all have something in common: they are conventionalized combinations, taken up and reproduced by speakers who have used them – or heard them used by others – before. In other words, they do not represent novel creations of individual language users, assembled from scratch on the basis of regular rules of grammar and semantics that operate on individual words. In this article, we will use the term *multi-word expressions* (MWEs) to collectively refer to these various kinds of sequences.[2]

MWEs have generated a great amount of interest in linguistics over the past few decades, spurred largely by researchers who realized that earlier linguistic approaches were generally ill-equipped to handle such sequences. While these earlier approaches did acknowledge that highly salient MWEs with unpredictable meanings (viz., idioms) must be stored, such non-compositionality was considered a rather marginal linguistic feature – indeed, rule-based regularity was thought to be the dominant motif of language. However, in what has become a foundational paper in MWE research, Pawley and Syder (1983) point to the subtlety with which conventionalization among sequences of words may appear. What they term "native-like selection" describes production choices that L1 speakers make but which L2 speakers struggle with. Specifically, native speakers do not just choose words on the basis of word-level semantics and syntax, whereby two synonyms would be equally valid productions in a phrasal formulation. For example, while *strong* and *powerful* are both adjectives that share at least one sense, L1 speakers produce *strong coffee* but not *powerful coffee*. That is, although both formulations ostensibly communicate the same meaning, only the *strong coffee* sequence "feels" native-like. It must be the case, then, that L1 speakers store representations across usage events that describe the specific combination of the word type *strong* with the word type *coffee*. And, crucially, note that *strong coffee* appears decomposable into individual semantic units and thus does not seem to be an idiom expected to be stored in memory.

Works such as Pawley and Syder's have helped to shift linguists' thinking that what is stored versus assembled may actually be a much larger proportion of discourse than originally thought. Indeed, a number of studies have now set out to count the density of MWEs in discourse (e.g., Erman and Warren 2000; Foster 2001; Biber et al. 2004). And while results vary considerably based on how they operationalize and count sequence formulaicity, most studies find that between one third and a half of sequences appear to instantiate dependencies between specific lexical types. Moreover, the types of MWEs that have been shown to make up

[1]The list of types of MWEs above is by no means exhaustive or clear-cut; however, this list is inspired by a useful taxonomy in Siyanova-Chanturia, Conklin, and Schmitt (2011).

[2]Numerous terms, with partially overlapping definitions, have been broadly used to refer to the same general collection of phenomena (terms including fixed expressions, formulaic expressions, n-grams, phraseologisms, and others).

discourse are not dominated by any one kind, ranging from the subtle collocational preferences of native speakers to well-known lexical compounds.

With this emergent appreciation for the extent of between-word formulaicity, various subfields have shifted attention to MWEs. These include the use of MWEs as the basis for the differentiation between varieties of the same language (Gries and Mukherjee 2010) and between genres within a single language (Biber et al. 2004); creating multi-word dictionary entries in lexicographic work (Sinclair 1987); development of native-like abilities in second language acquisition (e.g., Sinclair 1987; Simpson-Vlach and Ellis 2010); exploration of the role of MWEs in child acquisition (Bannard and Matthews 2008) and adult language processing (Bod 2009); and creating native-like speech in natural language generation (Lareau et al. 2011), among many others.

The increasing research foci on MWEs have been accompanied by the ongoing development of methods for the identification of such sequences in discourse. Unsurprisingly, the traditional method for such identification is through hand annotation. However, this method is slow, expensive, not necessarily objective, or replicable across raters, and it does not scale up well to large corpora. One important way of addressing these limitations is through automated computational approaches for the extraction of MWEs from corpora. These approaches typically generate a list of candidate multi-word structures from a corpus and then score and rank them according to some statistical metric of co-occurrence strength. Those items ranked highest represent the algorithm's best hypotheses for true MWEs, and those ranked lowest represent the algorithm's best hypotheses for what are not MWEs. Ultimately, these items must be hand curated to more or less of a degree, with the removal of erroneous results.

These algorithms vary along a number of dimensions relating to how MWEs are defined, counted, and extracted (issues that we return to in the next sections); thus, they will yield different lists of MWEs that they hypothesize in a given text. At the same time, they all rely on the premise that MWEs ought to be discoverable through word co-occurrence counts. This is because, over diachronic time, linguistic structures that are recurrently used become increasingly conventionalized in meaning and form; thus, conventionalization/formulaicity tends to correlate with usage frequency.

The current article presents an implemented algorithm that we have developed for the extraction of MWEs, entitled MERGE (Multi-word Expressions from the Recurrent Grouping of Elements)[3]. As we will discuss below, this algorithm differs from many traditional approaches to MWE extraction in that it identifies sequences of various sizes that may or may not include "gaps" in them. In this way, it is designed to be sensitive to the many different structural formats that MWEs can take in language, from sequences that are adjacent (e.g., *apple pie*) to discontinuous (e.g., *as ... as*), from those that are shorter to longer (e.g., *that's what she said*).

[3]Specifically, the algorithm was first developed in the first author's Ph.D. dissertation, which was co-supervised by the second author.

MERGE accomplishes this through a recurrent mechanism that builds on existing lexical association measures from the corpus linguistic literature on the extraction of MWEs. Furthermore, as we will demonstrate below, it offers a potentially superior method over other existing approaches that identify MWEs of different sizes, an issue we return to later.

In the next section, we return to the issue of defining MWEs, discussing terminological and definitional variation in the literature, and explaining how MWEs are operationalized in the present article; also, we discuss algorithmic approaches to MWE extraction, covering the role that lexical association measures have played in this research as well as how they are adapted to the current algorithm. In Sect. 3, we report two empirical studies to validate the performance of the algorithm using human participant ratings of model output. The first study in Sect. 3.1 compares human ratings of items extracted early by the algorithm to those extracted at later iterations, under the premise that, if MERGE is finding MWEs effectively, early-item ratings ought to be higher. The second study in Sect. 3.2 compares ratings assigned to output from MERGE to ratings assigned to output from another algorithm from the literature that identifies MWEs, in order to demonstrate that MERGE does offer competitive performance to an existing approach. Finally, in Sect. 4, we offer conclusions and directions for future research.

2 Multi-word Expressions: Their Definition and Extraction

2.1 The Definition of Multi-word Expressions

Numerous terminologies have been used in the literature to refer to formulaic, conventionalized word sequences: Wray (2002) identifies 60 terms, and her count is not exhaustive. Crucially, not all of these terms have been used to refer to exactly the same phenomena, and often the same term may be used in different works to refer to somewhat different phenomena. Despite variability in definitions, Gries (2008) identifies several different criteria that commonly appear across many definitions of formulaic language. He argues that the more researchers are consistent in defining their terms via a common set of criteria such as the ones he proposes, the easier it will be to compare studies. Thus, we define here our use of the term *multi-word expression* with reference to these criteria in an attempt to be explicit about the kinds of sequences that MERGE learns. In this discussion, we also note how the sequences that MERGE is tasked with identifying differ from (and are often more realistic/complete than) the kinds of sequences that more conventional extraction approaches are designed to identify.

Of the ways in which definitions of MWEs vary that Gries (2008) mentions, perhaps that which is most oft-cited in MWE research is the *role of semantic (non-)compositionality*. For some researcher, semantic non-compositionality (e.g., *kick the bucket* has nothing to with kicking or buckets) is a prerequisite for formulaicity. For others, whether or not a word sequence is compositional is a basis for categorizing word sequences into different types (e.g., idiomatic versus non-idiomatic formulaic language; see Conklin and Schmitt 2012). And still in other approaches, there may be no direct accounting for semantics at all; instead, frequency-based metrics may be the sole means for identifying MWEs. Since most corpora are not annotated with the kind of semantic information that would distinguish non-compositional from compositional sequences, it is this last approach that we adopt.

Gries (2008) also notes that definitions of formulaic language vary in terms of the *types of units that can make up a co-occurrence* and the *lexical and syntactic flexibility* among these units. The most prototypical type of MWE comprises two or more words that do not admit any variation or only admit variation at the level of differing inflections (though often researchers may work with lemmatized corpora to avoid such inflectional variation). Exceptions include, for example, Gries' (2008) definition of phraseologism, which includes co-occurrences between words and paradigmatic slots that accept any number of word types representing a lexical class (e.g., *as tall as* versus *as red as*, *he spilled the beans* versus *she spilled the beans*, etc.).

Sag et al. (2002) taxonomize such lexico-syntactic flexibility, distinguishing between fixed expressions, semifixed expressions, and flexible expressions. Fixed expressions include sequences such as *by and large*, ad hoc, and *Palo Alto*, and often exhibit lexico-syntactic irregularities. Semifixed expressions allow some inflectional variations and include many non-decomposable idioms, compound nominals, and proper names. Finally, syntactically flexible MWEs include verb-particle constructions, decomposable idioms, and light verb constructions. Admittedly, the theoretical inclusion of flexible slots offers a more complete picture of MWEs as elements that interact with and are embedded within larger syntactic phrasal and clausal structures. However, computationally accounting for paradigmatic flexibility within MWEs quickly becomes a much more complex grammar induction problem, which is beyond the scope of most collocation studies. Accordingly, the MWEs that MERGE is tasked with identifying for now comprise strict co-occurrences of word forms.

The remaining three criteria that Gries (2008) identifies are where extraction algorithms tend to vary the most. Two of these are the *number of units in the MWE* and the *syntagmatic distance between units*. Regarding the first of these, often corpus linguists just focus on bigrams, as they are easy to extract computationally and handle statistically. Regarding the second criterion, researchers tend to focus on sequences whose elements are strictly adjacent. However, real MWEs may in principle be of any length, and they may involve discontinuous sequences, and thus an ideal algorithm ought to be able to extract such variable-length, possibly discontinuous MWEs. Indeed, some existing research has developed techniques for extracting adjacent MWEs of variable lengths (e.g., Nagao and Mori 1994; Daudaravičius and Murcinkevičienė 2004; Gries and Mukherjee 2010; O'Donnell 2011), as well as MWEs of variable lengths containing gaps (e.g., Ikehara et al. 1996; Da Silva et al. 1999; Wible et al. 2006). Similarly, the MERGE algorithm is designed to extract variable-length sequences that are both continuous and discontinuous, and it is designed to do so in a way that improves upon existing approaches. It is important to note that MERGE's ability to include gaps in MWEs allows for spaces in which different lexical items of particular paradigms might be located, as discussed with regard to the *lexical and syntactic flexibility* criterion. However, MERGE does not directly learn anything about these paradigms.

Gries' (2008) final criterion is the *role of unit co-occurrence frequency* in defining a particular notion of formulaic language. Again, this is one of the criteria for which there is great variation among automated extraction techniques. As mentioned above, usage frequency is correlated with formulaicity. As such, direct corpus counts of sequence frequency may serve as a measure of MWE status (e.g., Biber et al. 2004), and some automatic extraction approaches are based on frequency counts (e.g., O'Donnell 2011). However, not all MWEs can be captured via frequency: idioms, for example, are typically low frequency yet clearly memorized; for example, an expression such as *blithering idiot(s)* occurs approximately once per 50 m words (in the Corpus of Contemporary American English) and yet is known to most native speakers of American English.

2.2 The Extraction of Multi-word Expressions

The identification of MWEs of different sizes and the use of lexical association measures present a paradox. On the one hand, most lexical association measures are designed for bigrams and do not scale to larger co-occurrences in obvious or uncontroversial manners. For this reason, the work that draws on these measures has tended to focus on such bigrams, neglecting interesting larger co-occurrences. One possibility of circumventing this problem is to use a simpler measure such as frequency, which is counted in the same way regardless of sequence length. However and as mentioned above, frequency counts alone may miss interesting co-occurrences that are low-frequency yet high-saliency, such as idioms. Still, assuming a particular algorithm were to manage a solution to this contradiction and could assign strength values to MWEs of different sizes, there is still the quandary of how to identify the correct size of a particular MWE. In other words, a high-scoring bigram such as *in spite* may simply be a part of a larger "true" MWE such as *in spite of*. Or, two adjacent high-scoring trigrams such as *be that as* and *as it may* may exhibit a one-word overlap such that the true MWE is the five-gram that spans them both. Simply extracting all 2- through *n*-grams and then scoring and ranking them will result in a list of many such cases. Thus, it would be desirable to develop an extraction approach whose ultimate output does not include such fragmentary cases.

In the next subsection, we provide a brief discussion of lexical association measures, given the central role they have played in MWE research in general and the role one measure plays in MERGE in particular. Then, in Sect. 2.2.1, we turn to the description of recent extraction techniques that address the issues that we have just raised in different ways.

Table 5.1 Schematic 2 × 2 table for co-occurrence statistics/association measures

	$\text{Word}_2 = \text{present}$	$\text{Word}_2 = \text{absent}$	Totals
$\text{Word}_1 = \text{present}$	obs: a exp: $(a + b) \times (a + c)/n$	obs: a exp: $(a + b) \times (b + d)/n$	$a + b$
$\text{Word}_1 = \text{absent}$	obs: a exp.: $(c + d) \times (a + c)/n$	obs: a obs: a	$c + d$
Totals	$a + c$	$b + d$	$a + b + c + d = n$

2.2.1 Traditional Lexical Association Measures

Numerous lexical association measures have been developed by corpus linguists to quantify the amount of statistical attraction between words in bigram relationships (Pecina (2009) reviews 80 separate measures). Most of these measures are based on *contingency tables*, such as the one in Table 5.1, which represents schematically the observed and expected frequencies of occurrence of the constituents of a bigram (or any bipartite collocation, for that matter) and their co-occurrence.

Generally, lexical association measures are based on various mathematical formulae that compare observed frequency cell value(s) to expected frequency cell value(s). Using an association measure's formula, one can calculate an association score for each bigram type; these scores may then be used to rank the bigrams in a corpus by strength. While each measure's scores represent different units, often a positive value will indicate statistical association between two words: that is, that the two words co-occur more often than might be expected by chance. Conversely, a negative value will indicate statistical repulsion, or that two words occur less frequently than might be expected by chance.

Of the measures that have been developed, some have emerged as more popular than others. For example, mutual information (*MI*) is among the most well-known association measure. However, *MI* and transitional probability – which is not usually considered a lexical association measure but nonetheless measures sequence strength – exhibit a similar problem. They rank very low-frequency, high-contingency bigrams too highly (e.g., a bigram in which both component words are hapaxes; see Daudaravičius and Murcinkevičienė 2004); alternatives such as MI^k fare somewhat better in this respect (see McEnery 2006, Evert 2009:1225). Another, and maybe the most popular, lexical association measure that has yielded quite good results (e.g., Wahl 2015) and does not appear oversensitive to very low frequencies is log likelihood (Dunning 1993), whose formula is given in (2).

(2) $\text{log likelihood} = 2\sum_{i=a}^{d} \text{obs} \times \log \frac{\text{obs}}{\text{exp}}$

Unlike other measures, log likelihood takes into account observed and expected values from all four frequency cells (a, b, c, and d) of the contingency table. It also provides a close approximation to Fisher's exact test (Evert 2009:1235), considered on mathematical grounds to be the best method for quantifying statistical association (yet its computational cost to implement makes it prohibitive for iterative applications like MERGE). Due to these strong credentials, log likelihood is the measure we use in the present implementation of MERGE[4]. One final point that should be made is that (2) will always result in positive values. Thus, in order for log likelihood scores to correspond to the convention in which positive values denote statistical attraction between words and negative values repulsion, the product of eq. 1 must be multiplied by -1 when the observed frequency of a bigram is less than the expected (following Evert 2009:1227).

2.2.2 Some Newer Developments

In this section, we discuss some newer developments in MWE extraction research. First, we discuss two studies that use a so-called lexical gravity approach; then, we turn to O'Donnell's (2011) adjusted frequency list; finally, we discuss work on discontinuous MWEs, focusing in particular on the recursive bigram approach by Wible et al. (2006).

Daudaravîĉius and Murcinkevîĉiené (2004) develop a new lexical association measure known as lexical gravity (*LG*). The distinctive feature of this measure is that, unlike all other measures used with at least some frequency, it takes the type frequency of the token frequencies (in particular in cell *b*) into account; see Gries (2012) for detailed exemplification. At its heart, *LG* is based on the sum of the forward and backward transitional probabilities (TPs) of a two-way co-occurrence. However, each TP is weighted by the type frequency (i.e., the number of different word types) that can occupy its outcome slot, given its cue. Thus, for a given (forward or backward) TP, there is a reward for promiscuity in possible outcomes and a punishment for faithfulness (this is because a high TP is more impressive when it occurs in the context of many possible outcomes).

While *LG*, like other association measures, is principally a two-way co-occurrence metric, Daudaravîĉius and Murcinkevîĉiené 2004 develop a technique for extending it to the identification of $n + 2$-grams. Their algorithm moves through the corpus incrementally and considers any uninterrupted sequence of bigrams with *LG* values exceeding 5.5 as constituting an MWE or *collocational chain* in their terminology (they do not motivate their choice of 5.5 as their threshold value, but at df $= 1$ this corresponds to a *p*-value of approximately 0.02). In a later paper, Gries and Mukherjee (2010) refine this technique by basing the collocational chain criterion on *mean LG*. Specifically, they extract *n*-grams of various lengths and score them on the basis of the mean *LG* of their component bigrams, discarding those *n*-grams with mean *LG*s below 5.5. Then, they proceed through the list, discarding *n*-grams that are contained by one or more $n + 1$-grams with a higher mean *LG* score. The resulting list constitutes their algorithm's hypothesis of the MWEs in the corpus.

[4]Note that while log likelihood is developed in Dunning (1993) as a lexical association measure, it is in fact a multiple of another measure known as the Kullback-Leibler (K-L) divergence from the field of information theory (Evert 2005). K-L divergence was not developed to quantify word co-occurrences, but rather to measure the difference between two discrete probability distributions that share the same domain.

Rather than adapting lexical association measures to co-occurrences beyond the bigram, another set of approaches circumvent this problem by employing frequency counts as a metric of MWE strength. One of the seminal works on MWE extraction, by Nagao and Mori 1994, takes this approach, as does the more recent adjusted frequency list (AFL) by O'Donnell (2011). This latter algorithm works by first identifying all *n*-grams up to some size threshold in a corpus. Next, only *n*-grams exceeding some frequency threshold are retained in the AFL along with their frequency (in his paper, the author set this frequency threshold to three). Then, for each *n*-gram, starting with those of threshold length and descending by order of length, the two component *n*-minus-1-grams are derived. Finally, the number of tokens in the frequency list of each *n*-minus-1-gram is decremented by the number of *n*-grams in which it is a component. Like the lexical gravity approaches, this procedure prevents the kinds of overlaps and redundancies that would result from a brute-force approach of simply extracting all *n*-grams of various sizes and then ranking them based on frequency. However, in using the AFL, there is the possibility that low-frequency, high-contingency MWEs would be ignored.

One drawback of these approaches is that, as implemented, they do not allow for discontinuous MWEs. Most corpus linguistic work has shied away from the challenges of the combinatorial explosion entailed by extracting MWEs with discontinuities. Notable exceptions include an early approach by Ikehara et al. (1996) (itself based on the work by Nagao and Mori), Da Silva et al.'s (1999) LocalMax algorithm, and an algorithm by Wible et al. (2006), all of which are capable of identifying both continuous and discontinuous MWEs. We will focus on this last approach, which also crucially differs from other approaches in that it does not generate a list of ranked MWEs hypotheses contained in a corpus. Instead, it is designed to find all of the MWEs that a given node word participates in (in this way, it is more akin to a concordancer). The algorithm represents what we will call a recursive bigram approach. Upon selection of a node word to be searched, the algorithm generates continuous and discontinuous bigrams within a specified window size around each token of the node word in the corpus; these bigrams consist of all those that have the node word as one of their elements. Next, the algorithm scores these bigrams on the basis of a lexical association measure (they use *MI*), and all those bigrams whose score exceeds a specified threshold are "merged" into a single representation. The algorithm then considers new continuous and discontinuous bigrams, in which one of the elements is one of the new, merged representations, and the other element is a single word within the window. The new bigrams are scored, and winners are chosen and merged. This progress iterates until no more bigrams exceeding the threshold are found. Ultimately, the algorithm generates a list of MWEs of various sizes that contain the original node word. Importantly, the model never has to calculate association strengths for co-occurrences larger than two elements, since one element will always be a word, and, after the first iteration, the other element will always be a word sequence containing the node word.

2.2.3 Co-occurrence Versus Grammar-Based MWE Extraction

The methods for MWE extraction discussed thus far are based on recurrent co-occurrences between word forms or, sometimes, lemmas. Furthermore, they are unsupervised: while gold standard lists of MWEs may be used a posteriori to evaluate algorithms' performance, there are not parameters of the algorithm trained on labels prior to evaluation. In contrast to this paradigm, a parallel line of research for the identification of MWEs has been pursued in the field of computational linguistics. While methods vary, these researchers prototypically use supervised approaches whereby sequence labelers and/or parsers are trained on a partition of a corpus that is enriched with additional features besides just the boundaries between word forms or lemmas (see, e.g., Spence et al. 2013, Constant et al. 2017 for an up-to-date survey). For example, these features may include parts of speech labels, syntactic dependencies, MWE tags, and morphological and frequency/statistical association information. Once training has converged, the algorithm is tested on another partition of the corpus in order to see how it can match the MWE tags (and possibly other features).

Research has suggested that these labeler- and parser-based supervised approaches achieve a higher level of precision and recall than *n*-gram-based approaches. That said, unsupervised co-occurrence-based approaches present a different domain of application. To the extent that they do not rely on a corpus already enriched with MWE and POS labels, syntactic dependencies, and other features, they may be applied in a much broader set of contexts – for example, for the case of smaller languages with few corpus resources or with texts from specialized domains. In many of these circumstances, while the set of POS and syntactic category types (if not tokens) may be exhaustively known, it is not necessarily the case that the set of MWE types are known. Thus, unsupervised co-occurrence-based approaches allow for the exploratory, bottom-up investigation of what MWEs might exist within a particular domain.

2.2.4 MERGE: A New Recursive Bigram Approach

Similar to the algorithm developed by Wible et al. (2006), the MERGE algorithm embodies a recursive bigram approach. But unlike this earlier work, our algorithm is designed to extract all MWEs in a corpus (not just those that contain a particular node word). It begins by extracting all bigram tokens in a corpus. These include adjacent bigrams, as well as bigrams with one or more words intervening, up to some user-defined discontinuity parameter (similar to Wible et al.'s use of a window). The tokens for each bigram type are counted, as are the tokens for each individual word type, and the total corpus size (in words) is tallied. Next, these values are used to calculate log likelihood scores. The highest-scoring bigram is selected as the winner, and it is merged into a single representation; that is, it is assigned a data structure representation equivalent to the representations of individual words (this differs from Wible and colleagues' approach, wherein multiple winners were chosen at an iteration on the basis of a threshold association value). We call these representations *lexemes*. At the next stage, all tokens of co-occurring word lexemes in the corpus that instantiate the winning bigram are replaced by instances of the new, merged representation. More specifically, if the winning bigram type is the combination of the lexeme "in" followed by a one-word gap and followed by the lexeme "of," the newly created lexeme would be "in _ of." Furthermore, at each point in the corpus where this co-occurrence is attested, the leftmost word position is populated with the new lexeme ("in" becomes "in _ of") and the other word positions in the co-occurrence (i.e., "of") are populated with placeholder objects that point to the leftmost word position of the co-occurrence.

Frequency information and bigram statistics must then be updated. New candidate bigrams are created through the co-occurrence in the corpus of individual word lexemes with tokens of the new merged lexeme. For example, the lexeme *in _ of* can now co-occur with *spite*, which occurs in the gap between *in* and *of*. Furthermore, certain existing candidate bigrams may have lost tokens. That is, some of these tokens may have partially overlapped with tokens of the winning bigram (i.e., they shared a particular word token). Since these word tokens in effect no longer exist, these candidates' frequency counts must be adjusted downward. For example, some or all of the occurrences of the individual word *in* followed by *spite* have ceased to exist, since many/all of the relevant tokens of *in* were swallowed up by the merge that created *in _ of*. And because of this, the frequency of the individual word types found in the winner must be reduced by the number of winning bigram tokens. Finally, the corpus frequency has decreased, since individual words have been consumed by two-word sequences. After these adjustments in frequency information have been made, new bigram strengths can be calculated.

The cycle then iteratively repeats from the point at which a winning bigram is chosen above, and this iteration continues until the lexical association strength of the winning bigram reaches some minimum cutoff threshold. After cycle cutoff, the output of the algorithm is a corpus, parsed in terms of MWEs, and a list of lexemes, from individual words to MWEs of different sizes, with and without gaps.

Because the input to candidate bigrams at later iterations may be output from previous iterations, MERGE can grow MWEs unrestricted in size, which is similar to the Wible et al. (2006) algorithm. Another key difference, however, is that one element of their candidate bigrams must always be a single word and the other a word sequence (at least after the first iteration, where both elements are single words). In contrast, at later iterations, MERGE can choose a winning bigram that comprises two single words, a single word and a word sequence, or two word sequences. Moreover, assuming a sufficiently sized gap parameter, one element may in principal occur inside the gap of another element. Even more unusual scenarios are possible: *as _ matter* and *a _ of fact* could be interleaved to form *as a matter of fact*. Thus, there are many possible paths of successive merges that result in a particular MWEs, provided that the distance between the leftmost words of the two elements of a bigram never exceeds the discontinuity parameter.

Thus, MERGE sits at the vanguard in terms of MWE extraction research in that it identifies MWEs that are co-occurrences of (dis)continuous words of various lengths, on the basis of statistical measures of lexical association.

3 Empirical Evaluation of the Algorithm

It is necessary to determine whether MERGE does in fact do a reasonable job of identifying MWEs. In this section, we report two different empirical studies. In Sect. 3.1, we discuss a study in which human participants rated sequences extracted by the algorithm for how well these sequences reflect "true" MWEs. Specifically, we are testing the hypothesis that the point in time when MERGE labels an expression a MWE can distinguish MWEs that are highly formulaic from MWEs that are not. After that, in Sect. 3.2, we discuss another such rating study; this time, however, the output of MERGE is compared to the output of a different automated MWE extraction approach from the literature, the AFL, to test the hypothesis that MWEs returned by MERGE will score higher in formulaicity than MWEs returned by the AFL approach.

3.1 Rating Study 1: "Good" vs. "Bad" MWEs

In this study, we explore how human participants rate MWEs that differ along two crucial dimensions. The first of these dimensions is captured in a binary variable BINRANK, *early* vs. *late*, which states when during MERGE's application a MWE is identified: early (which, if MERGE is successful, should be MWEs that are rated as highly formulaic) or late (which should be MWEs that should not be rated as highly formulaic).

The second dimension is captured in a numeric variable SIZE which could take on values from 2 to 5 and just provides the number of lexical constituents of the MWE. In Sect. 3.1.1, we discuss how the MWEs we used in the experiment were obtained; in Sect. 3.1.2, we describe how the experiment was designed and undertaken; in Sect. 3.1.3, we discuss how the results were analyzed statistically; in Sect. 3.1.4, we present the results of the statistical analysis, and in Sect. 3.1.5, we provide an interim summary and discussion of this first case study.

3.1.1 Materials

The input data for the algorithm comprised two corpora: the Santa Barbara Corpus of Spoken American English (SBC; Du Bois, Chafe, Meyer, and Thompson 2000; Du Bois, Chafe, Meyer, Thompson, and Martey 2003; Du Bois and Englebretson 2004; 2005) and the spoken component of the Canadian subcorpus of the International Corpus of English (ICE-Canada Spoken; Newman and Columbus 2010). SBC includes about 250,000 words, while ICE-Canada Spoken includes about 450,000, for a combined total of 700,000 words.

To maximize the likelihood that study participants would be familiar with the MWEs that appear, it was decided to use corpora that comprise recent North American English, since the participants are young college students in the USA. Furthermore, it was decided to use spoken language data that span a variety of discourse genres (the files of the corpora include face-to-face and telephone conversations, academic lectures, religious sermons, political debates, business meetings, radio programs, and many others). The greater formality of written language means that it is more likely to contain low-frequency, unfamiliar word combinations.[5]

These criteria greatly limited the candidate corpora, so we decided to combine two smaller corpora to generate as large a data set as possible. Note that, although more than half of the words in the combined corpus are from Canadian speech, while the study participants are from the USA, the differences between these two varieties are relatively minute compared to the differences between, say, US and British varieties (the reason why the ten million word spoken component of the British National Corpus was not used).

The formatting of both corpora was then standardized. All tags and transcription characters that were not part of the lexical representation of the words themselves were removed, including markers of overlap in talk, laughter, breathing, incomprehensible syllables, pauses, and other non-lexical vocalizations, among other features.

Following corpus preprocessing, the MERGE algorithm was run on the data set. The maximum gap size threshold was set to one – that is, the algorithm could acquire MWEs with one or more gaps within them, provided that these gaps were no longer than one word long. The algorithm was run for 20,000 iterations. Bigrams that span a boundary between turns-at-talk were not permitted.

Next, output MWEs were selected for use as experimental stimuli. These included the first 40 and last 40 merged items for each size of MWE in terms of the number of words that they contained, from MWEs of two words to MWEs of five words. While the model did extract sequences of six or more words, these were relatively few in number, so a maximum size of five words was chosen. Thus, 320 different MWE types were selected, with half belonging to an *early* bin and half to a *late* bin.

---

[5]This assumption that written language exhibits a greater lexical diversity than the often more repetitive, simpler topics kind of language you find in spoken data (especially in conversation) is widely held and supported, for instance, by a quick computation of lexical diversity statistics in the ICE-GB. Guiraud's measure of lexical diversity returns a value of approximately 64.3 for all the written data in ICE-GB, which is completely different than the mean of 500 random samples of the same number of words from the spoken data without replacement, mean = 41.2, IQR = 0.14.

3.1.2 Experimental Design

Four different versions of the rating survey were then created, each containing 80 MWEs. Each version included 10 two-word MWEs from the early bin, 10 two-word MWEs from the late bin, 10 three-word MWEs from the early bin, and so forth. Each group of 10 words was selected at random, without replacement, from all the MWEs that exhibited the same bin identity and were of the same size. Five copies of each version of the survey were then created (with stimuli ordered randomized within each copy), for a total of 20 surveys. Each stimulus item was also accompanied by an example utterance sourced from the corpus that contained the item, so that study participants had a sense of the use of the candidate MWE in context.

Next, the survey instructions were prepared. As discussed in Sect. 2, there are various criteria involved in defining/identifying MWEs, which differ from study to study. However, as we have mentioned, a common thread among different definitions and types of MWEs is that they are maintained in and reused from memory across usage events, rather than constructed on line from regular rules. In order to tap into nonspecialist intuitions about this notion, the instructions asked participants to rate sequences, on a seven-point Likert scale, for how well they represented *common, reusable chunks* (with seven indicating strong agreement). The instructions were supplemented with both good and bad examples of common, reusable chunks, based on the opinion of the researcher. These examples were sourced from the MERGE output and were not included as stimulus items.

Finally, 20 participants were recruited from introductory linguistics courses at the University of California, Santa Barbara. Each participant was placed in a quiet room by themselves and given as much time as they needed to complete the survey.

3.1.3 Statistical Analysis

The judgment data were analyzed with what is currently the state of the art for psycholinguistic data with dependent numeric (or potentially ordinal) variables, a linear mixed-effects model; we used the software language and environment R (R Core Team 2016) with the packages lmer (Bates et al. 2015) for the overall model selection process, lmerTest (Kuznetsova et al. 2016) to obtain *p*-values (based on Satterthwate's approximations), as well as MuMIn (Barton 2015) to obtain R^2 values for our regression models (Nakagawa and Schielzeth 2010, Johnson 2014). The dependent variable in our regression model was RATING, i.e., those ratings provided by the subjects. As independent variables, we entered the above-mentioned predictors SIZE (as an orthogonal polynomial to the second degree) and BINRANK as well as their interaction. The random-effects structure we used was the maximal random-effects structure that converged without warnings (following Barr et al. 2013): varying intercepts for every *n*-gram and every experimental subject as well as slopes for SIZE and BINRANK for every *n*-gram and every subject.

Note that this approach to evaluation differs from many of the approaches adopted in the literature on supervised MWE identification. There, algorithm

Table 5.2 Results for the fixed-effects part of the regression model (REML)

Predictor	coef	se	df	t	$p_{2\text{-tailed}}$
Intercept	5.69	0.16	29.6	34.86	$<10^{-15}$
SIZE (polynomial 1)	−26.26	4.13	129.6	−6.36	$<10^{-8}$
SIZE (polynomial 2)	−13.04	2.85	162.5	−4.57	$<10^{-5}$
BINRANK: *early* → *late*	−3.87	0.2	31	−19.17	$<10^{-15}$
SIZE (polynomial 1): BINRANK	15.88	4.93	178.6	3.22	0.0015
SIZE (polynomial 2): BINRANK	11.66	3.92	322.2	2.98	0.0031

performance is compared against MWE labels/decisions as to whether a particular sequence is or is not an MWE provided by human subjects, which are considered to be to be the gold standard. Here, we make no such Boolean either-or claims but use scalar information instead. Because of this methodological choice, the conventional Boolean-based evaluation metrics of "precision" and "recall" are not available, and instead we use regression to assess the degree of correlation between human ratings and algorithm performance.

3.1.4 Results

The results of the linear mixed-effects model indicated a significant correlation (LR chi-squared 87.08, df $= 5$, $p < 10^{-15}$, from a ML-comparison to a model without fixed effects) with a high/strong overall effect: R^2marginal, the R^2-value that quantifies the amount of variance explained by the fixed effects, is 0.643, and all fixed effects entered into the model reached standard levels of significance; see Table 5.2 for the corresponding results.

Compared to the above-mentioned fixed-effects, the random-effects structure, while having some effect, did less in terms of variance explanation: R^2conditional, the R^2-value that quantifies the amount of variance explained by both fixed and random effects, is 0.84, and the main random-effects contributions were made by both varying intercepts and by the different GRAM slopes for BINRANK; the product-moment correlation between the observed ratings and the one predicted by our model is $r = 0.93$.

Figure 5.1 is a visual effects-plot representation of both our fixed- and random-effects results. On the x-axis, we show the predictor SIZE, on the y-axis the predicted judgments by the experimental participants (averaged across MWEs). Each thin blue and red line represents a single participant's regression line for the BINRANK, *early*, and BINRANK, *late* data, respectively (highlighting the individual variation quantified by the random-effects structure), whereas the red and blue confidence bands indicate the impact the interaction of the two fixed effects has on the predicted judgments.

The main effect of BINRANK, *early* vs. *late,* is the most crucial finding in this experiment: the (blue) early MWEs, the ones hypothesized to be highly formulaic, do indeed have highly significantly higher overall ratings than the (red) late MWEs,

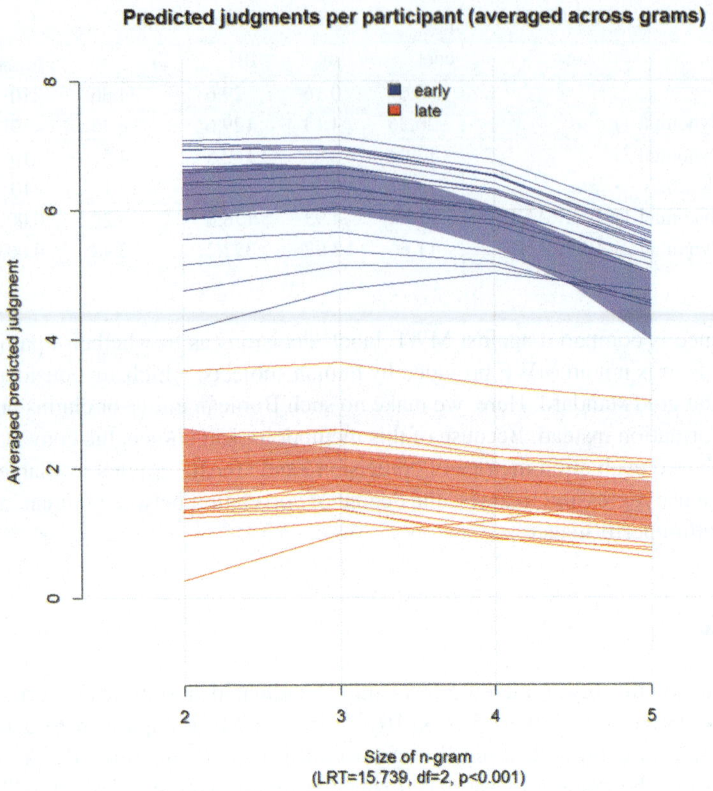

Fig. 5.1 The interaction of poly(SIZE, 2): BINRANK

which confirms the main hypothesis formulated above. The main effect of SIZE, on the other hand, consists of the expected weak negative correlation such that the longer the MWE, the lower its ratings. This is to some extent a reflection of the fact that the longer an expression, the less likely it is to indeed be a stored unit in the subjects' mental lexicons rather than "creatively" assembled on the spot and the less likely subjects were to recognize it as an expression they would give a high rating. This finding is compatible with the frequencies of lengths of MWEs in corpora: the spoken component of the British National Corpus contains >65 K MWEs of length 2, ≈10.5 K MWEs of length 3, 675 MWEs of length 4, and 10 of length 5.

While the main effects just discussed are relatively straightforward to interpret, they also participate in a highly significant interaction. Crucially for the purposes of the present paper, the interaction is of such a nature that it does not negate (any part of) the effect of BINRANK. Instead, it reflects the fact that MWEs returned late by MERGE do not decrease much in formulaicity as they become longer: we believe that, in some sense, this is little more than a floor effect, and in general, there's a negative effect of SIZE such that longer MWEs are less formulaic than shorter ones. Since MWEs with BINRANK (*late*) are already also much less formulaic than those with BINRANK (*early*), there is just not that much "judgment space" to decrease to, as is evidenced by the fact that the fixed-effects confidence interval for the red regression line is not only compatible with a straight and completely horizontal regression line but when SIZE = 5 is very close to the minimally possible judgment value of 1.

3.1.5 Interim Summary

The main finding of our first experiment is that the MERGE algorithm does indeed seem successful in identifying highly formulaic MWEs at an early stage of its application and returns less formulaic ones at a later stage (when association strengths decrease). This finding is compatible with our above hypothesis and, thus, constitutes a first piece of encouraging evidence in favor of MERGE. However, more evidence is needed to begin to make a solid case for MERGE, and we will provide more evidence in the next section. Specifically, in Sect. 3.2, we contrast the MWEs returned by MERGE with those of a competing proposal, namely, O'Donnell's AFL discussed above in Sect. 2.2.2.

3.2 Rating Study 2: AFL vs. MERGE

One of the major dimensions along which algorithms vary, as discussed in Sect. 2, is how they quantify the statistical strength of MWEs in order to rank MWEs from "better" to "worse." Many approaches, such as MERGE, use lexical association measures, which take into account various pieces of frequency information relevant to a target word co-occurrence. The drawback of such measures is that they have typically been limited to two-way co-occurrences and are thus not viable for comprehensively finding longer MWEs in a corpus (such as *it goes without saying*); this is because of the facts that just about all measures are based on co-occurrence tables of the type shown in Table 5.1 and that it is not obvious how to compute the expected frequencies of more than two words (since complete conditional independence is ridiculously anticonservative, see Gries 2010:275). The collocational chain approaches in Daudaravičius and Murcinkevičienė (2004) and Gries and Mukherjee (2010) and the recursive bigram approaches of Wible et al. (2006) and MERGE are innovative in their abilities to overcome this limitation. An alternative, however, to dealing with this would be to use a measure that was not limited to two-way co-occurrences, such as simple frequency counts.

This is precisely what another algorithm from the literature, the adjusted frequency list (AFL), does (O'Donnell 2011). Under this approach, candidate MWEs are ranked based simply on how often they occur. But remember that certain word sequences may represent true MWEs yet be low frequency. Idioms are a prototypical example of such sequences. We would thus anticipate a frequency-based approach such as the AFL to fail to identify many good MWEs that follow this pattern.

Conversely, lexical association measures are designed to be able to find such low-frequency yet high-contingency sequences, so an approach like MERGE that has adapted such a measure to sequences beyond bigrams ought to be able to not only find low-frequency MWEs but ones of various sizes. In this section, we thus compare MERGE and the AFL in another rating experiment in order to test the hypothesis that an approach such as MERGE that scales lexical association up to co-occurrences greater than 2 is superior to an approach that obviates this by using frequency, which is not inherently restricted to bigrams.

A final note should be made regarding discontinuities in MWEs. Remember that MERGE is designed to be able to find them; the AFL is not. Already, then, it can be claimed that MERGE offers something beyond the AFL in that it identifies an additional format of possible MWE. The present study will therefore be limited to comparing the performances of the algorithms in their ability to find MWEs with purely adjacent words. To this end, MERGE's max gap size parameter will be set here to zero.

3.2.1 Materials

The same corpora used in experiment 1 were also used here, with the same preprocessing procedures. Next, the algorithms were run and the top 1000-ranked items from the output of each were selected for further consideration. In the case of MERGE, this involved simply running the algorithm for 1000 iterations. In the case of the AFL, the minimum frequency threshold was set to 5 and the 1000 items with highest frequencies were selected. We then decided to focus on the MWEs that the two algorithms did not agree on rather than the MWEs that they had in common. Thus, two groups of items were created: the first group comprised those items found in the AFL output but not in the MERGE output; the second group comprised those items found in the MERGE output but not in the AFL output; this means the two lists do not share any items (and the overlap of the lists is not relevant since we are comparing the algorithms on the basis of an external "gold standard," the subjects' ratings). This allowed a highly tractable examination of how the respective performances of the two algorithms contrasted, as stimulus items fell into one of two categories.[6] The two groups of disjunctive output contained 180 items each. An even distribution of sampling from across the range of items was

[6] Note that there would have been difficulties in comparing the performance of the algorithms on the basis of the output that they had in common (i.e., by seeing which algorithm's ranking of output best correlated with participant-assigned ratings of this output). Since the strength metrics used to rank output were different for each model, the algorithm-assigned strength values would have to have been rank-ordered to make them comparable across algorithms. But the fact that the AFL is based on integer frequency means that there are numerous ties, whereas the log likelihood decimal values used by MERGE make for virtually no ties (at least at higher scores). Thus, the rank order distributions of the two model outputs were intractably different.

Table 5.3 Random sampling of output from AFL and MERGE

AFL		MERGE	
He is	*Well it*	*Auto reverse*	*Good afternoon*
And just	*They all*	*In the middle of*	*Melissa Soligo*
But if you	*And how*	*We need*	*They weren't*
Because the	*To their*	*To make sure*	*Must have been*
And this	*Of it*	*Square root*	*Next week*
And I think	*A real*	*I want you*	*A good idea*
It the	*Says the*	*You think*	*I wanted to*
Get a	*With that*	*Kind of thing*	*We'll see*
Before the	*There and*	*Let us*	*Thanks very much*
What kind of	*So this*	*Major depression*	*A great*

achieved by partitioning the two rank-ordered item groups into 10 bins and then randomly sampling 18 items from each bin. These items were then used in our experimental design.

3.2.2 Experimental Design

On the basis of the items sampled as described above, groups of stimuli for the surveys were created, with each group containing 45 items sampled randomly without replacement from each of the two groups of 180 items above. Thus, each survey contained 90 items – 45 generated by MERGE and 45 generated by the AFL. In Table 5.3, we provide a random sampling of 20 stimuli sourced from the 180 AFL items and 20 sourced from the 180 MERGE items.

One can immediately appreciate the qualitative difference between many of the items in these two lists. While the high-frequency sequences represented in the AFL output comprise many combinations of function words, the MERGE output comprises many sequences combining function and content words. The combinations include structures such as noun phrases (*a good idea*) or compound nouns (*square root*), compound prepositions (*in the middle of*), whole utterances (*thanks very much*), or phrasal verbs (*to make sure*), among others. Furthermore, while these combinations may be lower overall in frequency, their component words are mutually contingent. This type of relationship of mutual contingency is precisely the statistical pattern that lexical association measures like log likelihood are designed to capture.

At the next stage (and as in the first study), 20 surveys were created, including 5 of each version, each to be rated by a single participant. Again, the order of presentation of stimulus items for each survey was randomized, and each stimulus item was accompanied by an utterance sourced from the corpus containing that stimulus item, so that study participants had a sense of the use of the candidate MWEs in context. Pilot testing revealed that the ratings assigned across the two stimulus groups did not differ significantly, despite the apparent qualitative difference in the stimulus patters seen in Table 5.3. It is possible that the instructions to identify *common, reusable chunks* are to blame for this result. While they yielded successful results in the first study, the instructions did not appear effective here; this may be because they failed to tap into intended intuitions about memorization. For example, the idea of *commonness* may trigger intuitions about frequency rather than memory, and *reusability* may trigger notions about utility. To try to more explicitly target intuitions about memorization, the instructions were altered. In the new version, study participants were asked to rate sequences based on whether, in their opinion, they represented a *complete unit of vocabulary*. The hope was that participants' understanding of the notion of vocabulary would be roughly analogous to the linguistic notion of a lexicon, since these US students would have grown up learning vocabulary lists in spelling classes, etc. Again as in the first study, 20 participants were recruited from an introductory linguistics course at the University of California, Santa Barbara. Each participant was placed in a quiet room by themselves and given as much time as they needed to complete the survey.

3.2.3 Statistical Analysis

The data were analyzed with a linear mixed-effects model as outlined above for experiment 1. In this case study, the dependent variable was again RATING, i.e., the numerical rating provided by subjects for MWEs; the independent variable was the binary variable ORIGIN, which specified from which list of MWEs – AFL vs. MERGE – the rated MWE was from (recall that we used items that were returned by only one algorithm). As above, the random-effects structure was maximal, including varying intercepts and slopes for both subjects and MWEs.

3.2.4 Results

The linear mixed-effects model we fitted resulted in a significant fit (LR chi-squared = 5, df = 1, $p = 0.0254$, from a ML-comparison to a model without fixed effects) but not a particularly strong correlation: R^2marginal = 0.02 and R^2conditional = 0.37; see Table 5.4 for the corresponding results.

As is obvious from the above statistics, the overall effect is weak – the product-moment correlation between the observed ratings and the one predicted by our model is $r = 0.68$ – and the random-effects structure explains more of the variance than the fixed effects. We visualize the findings in Fig. 5.2. On the x-axis, we

Table 5.4 Results for the fixed-effects part of the regression model (REML)

Predictor	coef	se	df	t	$p_{1\text{-tailed}}$
Intercept	3.93	0.27	19.7	14.6	<10–11
ORIGIN: *AFL* → *MERGE*	0.59	0.25	22.8	2.31	0.0151

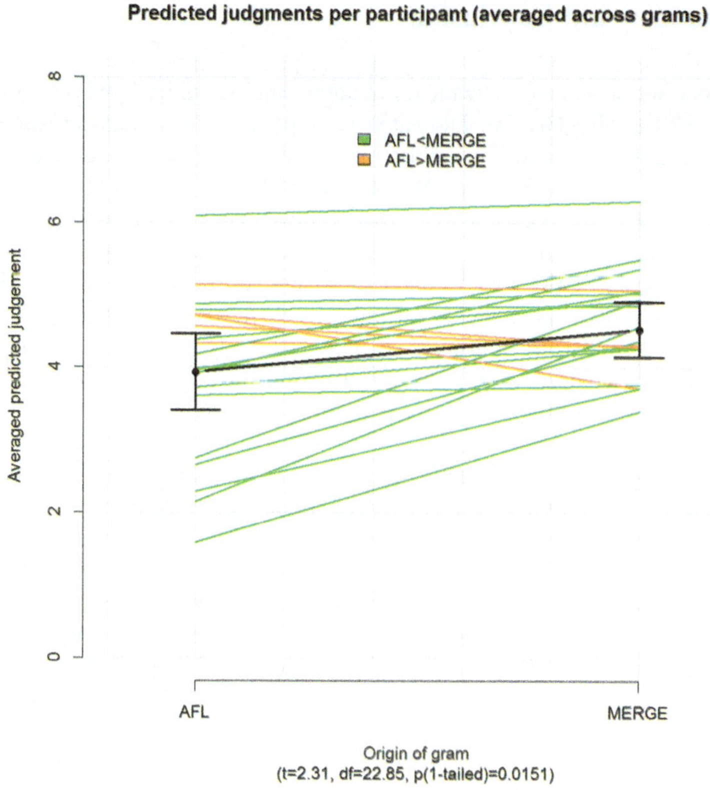

Fig. 5.2 The main effect of ORIGIN

represent the two levels of ORIGIN, on the *y*-axis the predicted judgments by the experimental participants (averaged across MWEs). Each green and orange line represents a single participant's regression line; a green line represents a participant's predicted median ratings for MWEs from the MERGE list, which are higher than those for the AFL list, an orange line represents the opposite relation, and the black points/lines (with confidence intervals) indicate the overall effect of ORIGIN.

The main effect of ORIGIN provides support for the hypothesized usefulness of the MERGE algorithm. While the effect is not strong and variable across subjects and MWEs, there is a significant difference such that the randomly sampled MWEs from the MERGE algorithm score higher average formulaicity judgments than the randomly sampled MWEs from the AFL algorithm. Given the small effect size, the evidence is not conclusive but nonetheless compatible with our hope/expectation of MERGE outperforming the AFL approach. In the next section, we will present our conclusions.

4 Discussion and Conclusion

In this paper, we presented a new recursive algorithm to identify MWEs in corpora, which we called MERGE. We motivated its application and characteristics and, more importantly, attempted to validate it in two experimental ways. In a first experiment, we demonstrated that MWEs returned by MERGE early, as predicted by MERGE's design, indeed score higher in formulaicity than MWEs returned by MERGE late, a robust main effect that is largely unqualified by an interaction with the size of an MWE. In a second experiment, we demonstrated that MWEs returned by MERGE score higher in formulaicity than MWEs returned by the AFL algorithm. While both case studies are small and can only begin to set the stage for the large and comprehensive set of tests that will ultimately be necessary for any new corpus-based algorithm, we interpret these first two significant results as good initial support for MERGE.

In terms of methodological implications, MERGE's performance provides further evidence for the effectiveness of lexical association measures in identifying meaningful word co-occurrences, especially compared to the use of raw frequency counts, as in the AFL. While the AFL found many high-frequency, low-contingency strings which do not obviously represent stored, meaningful units, MERGE was much more effective in its ability to single out salient sequences (i.e., sequences that occur more often than may be expected based on their individual word frequencies), a hallmark of lexical association measures. Furthermore, MERGE's performance exemplifies one effective way of scaling up lexical association measures to co-occurrences beyond the bigram. While the current study speaks to the good performance of the log likelihood association measure in this implementation, further work is needed to determine whether other association measures, such as the widely used *MI*-score, or newer measures such as *LG* (which includes type frequencies) or ΔP (which is directional, see Gries 2013), likewise yield good results when implemented in MERGE.

The MERGE algorithm offers a relatively simple approach that harnesses the proven potency of lexical association measures, and adapts them to MWEs of various sizes, with and without gaps. But MWEs are not merely crystallized sequences of words – the "slots" within them, or at their edges, may allow some (limited) set of words (i.e., a part-of-speech category) to fill them. In the future, it would be desirable if MERGE could be adapted to not only learn where the gaps were, but also what word paradigms might fill them; specifically, what the set of types is as well as their frequency distribution and maybe entropy. Furthermore, since members of the same paradigm may comprise different numbers of words, it would also be desirable if MERGE could be adapted to recognize identical word sequences containing gaps of different sizes as instantiating the same MWE (e.g., *as _ as* in *as funny as* versus *as __ as* in *as truly hilarious as*).

Conventionalized, memorized, multi-word sequences represent an important component in modern language sciences research, both at the level of cognitive and grammatical theory as well as in the applied domain of computer technologies. Being able to identify them automatically, using the explosion of corpus resources that are ever more available, is an increasingly important goal for researchers in various disciplines. The MWEs extracted by MERGE, which exhibit strong similarities to humanlike knowledge of formulaic language, indicate that this algorithm is a powerful tool for such work.

References

Bannard, C., & Matthews, D. (2008). Stored word sequences in language learning: The effect of familiarity on children's repetition of four-word combinations. *Psychological Science, 19*, 241–248.

Barr, D. J., Levy, R., Scheepers, C., & Tily, H. J. (2013). Random effects structure for confirmatory hypothesis testing: Keep it maximal. *Journal of Memory and Language, 68*(3), 255–278.

Barton, K. (2015). MuMin: Multi-model inference. *R package version, 1*(13), 4 http://cran.r-project.org/web/packages/MuMIn/index.html.

Bates, D., Maechler, M., Bolker, B., & Walker, S. (2015). Fitting linear mixed-effects models using lme4. *Journal of Statistical Software, 67*(1), 1–48.

Biber, D., Conrad, S., & Cortes, V. (2004). If you look at ...: Lexical bundles in university teaching and textbooks. *Applied Linguistics, 25*(3), 371–405.

Bod, R. (2009). From exemplar to grammar: A probabilistic analogy-based model of language learning. *Cognitive Science, 33*(5), 752–793.

Conklin, K., & Schmitt, N. (2012). The processing of formulaic language. *Annual Review of Applied Linguistics, 32*(1), 45–61.

Constant, M., Eryigit, G., Monti, J., van der Plas, L., & Ramisch, C. (2017). Michael, and Amalia Todirascu. *Multiword Expression Processing: A Survey. Computational Linguistics., 43*(4), 837–892.

Da, S., Joaquin, F., Dias, G., Guilloré, S., & Pereira Lopes, J. G. (1999). Using LocalMax algorithm for the extraction of contiguous and non-contiguous multiword lexical units. *Proceedings of the 9th Portuguese Conference on Artificial Intelligence: Progress in Artificial Intelligence*, 849–849.

Daudaravičius, V., & Murcinkevičiene, R. (2004). Gravity counts for the boundaries of collocations. *International Journal of Corpus Linguistics, 9*(2), 321–348.

Du Bois, J. W., & Englebretson, R. (2004). *Santa Barbara corpus of spoken American English, part 3*. Philadelphia: Linguistic Data Consortium.

Du Bois, J. W., Chafe, W. L., Meyers, C., Thompson, S. A., & Martey, N. (2003). *Santa Barbara corpus of spoken American English, part 2*. Philadelphia: Linguistic Data Consortium.

Du Bois, J. W., & Englebretson, R. (2005). *Santa Barbara corpus of spoken American English, part 4*. Philadelphia: Linguistic Data Consortium.

Du Bois, J. W., Chafe, W. L., Meyers, C., & Thompson, S. A. (2000). *Santa Barbara corpus of spoken American English, part 1*. Philadelphia: Linguistic Data Consortium.

Dunning, T. (1993). Accurate methods for the statistics of surprise and coincidence. *Computational Linguistics, 19*(1), 61–74.

Erman, B., & Warren, B. (2000). The idiom principle and the open choice principle. *Text, 20*(1), 29–62.

Evert, S. (2005). The statistics of word co-occurrences: Word pairs and collocations. *Ph. D. Dissertation. Universität Stuttgart.*

Evert, S. (2009). Corpora and collocations. In A. Lüdeling & M. Kytö (Eds.), *Corpus linguistics: An international handbook* (Vol. 2, pp. 1212–1248). Berlin & New York: Mouton de Gruyter.

Foster, P. (2001). Rules and routines: A consideration of their role in the task-based language production of native and non-native speakers. In M. Bygate, P. Skehan, & M. Swain (Eds.), *Researching pedagogic tasks: Second language learning, teaching, and testing* (pp. 75–93). Harlow: Longman.

Green, S., de Marneffe, M.-C., Bauer, J., & Manning, C. D. (2013). Parsing models for identifying multiword expressions. *Computational Linguistics, 39*(1), 195–227.

Gries, S. T. (2008). Phraseology and linguistic theory: A brief survey. In S. Granger & F. Meunier (Eds.), *Phraseology: An interdisciplinary perspective* (pp. 3–25). Amsterdam: John Benjamins.

Gries, S. T. (2010). Useful statistics for corpus linguistics. In A. Sánchez & M. Almela (Eds.), *A mosaic of corpus linguistics: Selected approaches* (pp. 269–291). Peter Lang: Frankfurt am Main.

Gries, S. T. (2012). Frequencies, probabilities, association measures in usage-/exemplar-based linguistics: Some necessary clarifications. *Studies in Language, 36*(3), 477–510.

Gries, S. T. (2013). 50-something years of work on collocations: What is or should be next .... *International Journal of Corpus Linguistics, 18*(1), 137–165.

Gries, S. T., & Mukherjee, J. (2010). Lexical gravity across varieties of English: An ICE-based study of *n*-grams in Asian Englishes. *International Journal of Corpus Linguistics, 15*(4), 520–548.

Ikehara, S., Shirai, S., & Uchino, H. (1996). A statistical method for extracting uninterrupted and interrupted collocations from very large corpora. *Proceedings of the 16e Conference on Computational linguistics, 1*, 574–579.

Johnson, P. C. D. (2014). Extension of Nakagawa and Schielzeth's R2GLMM to random slopes models. *Methods in Ecology and Evolution, 5*(9), 944–946.

Kuznetsova, A., Brockhoff, P. B., & Christensen, R. H. B.. (2016). lmerTest: Tests in linear mixed effects models. R package version 2.0–30. https://CRAN.R-project.org/package=lmerTest

Lareau, F., Dras, M., Börschinger, B., & Dale, R. (2011). Collocations in multilingual natural language generation: Lexical functions meet lexical functional grammar. In *Proceedings of ALTA'11* (pp. 95–104).

McEnery, T. (2006). *Swearing in English: Bad language, purity and power from 1586 to the present. Abington*. New York: Routledge.

Nagao, M., & Mori, S. (1994). A new method of n-gram statistics for large number of n and automatic extraction of words and phrases from large text data of Japanese. Proceedings of the. In *15thconference on computational linguistics* (pp. 611–615).

Nakagawa, S., & Schielzeth, H. (2010). Repeatability for Gaussian and non-Gaussian data: A practical guide for biologists. *Biological Reviews, 85*(4), 935–956.

Newman, J., & Columbus, G. (2010). *The international Corpus of English – Canada*. Edmonton, Alberta: University of Alberta.

O'Donnell, M. B. (2011). The adjusted frequency list: A method to produce cluster-sensitive frequency lists. *ICAME Journal, 35*, 135–169.

Pawley, A., & Syder, F. H. (1983). Two puzzles for linguistic theory: Nativelike selection and nativelike fluency. In J. Richards & R. Schmidt (Eds.), *Language and communication* (pp. 191–225). London: Longman.

Pecina, P. (2009). *Lexical association measures: Collocation extraction*. Prague: Charles University.

R Core Team. (2016). *R: A language and environment for statistical computing*. Vienna: R Foundation for Statistical Computing.

Sag, I. A., Baldwin, T., bond, F., Copestake, A., & Flickinger, D. (2002). *Multiword expressions: A pain in the neck for NLP. Proceedings of the third international conference on intelligent text processing and computational linguistics* (pp. 1–15). Mexico City.

Simpson-Vlach, R., & Ellis, N. (2010). An academic formulas list. *Applied Linguistics, 31*(4), 487–512.

Sinclair, J. (1987). *Collins COBUILD English language dictionary*. Ann Arbor: Collins.

Siyanova-Chanturia, A., Conklin, K., & Schmitt, N. (2011). Adding more fuel to the fire: An eye-tracking study of idiom processing by native and non-native speakers. *Second Language Research, 27*(2), 251–272.
Wahl, A. (2015). Intonation unit boundaries and the storage of bigrams: Evidence from bidirectional and directional association measures. *Review of Cognitive Linguistics, 13*(1), 191–219.
Wible, D., Kuo, C.-H., Chen, M.-C., Tsao, N.-L., & Hung, T.-F. (2006). *A computational approach to the discovery and representation of lexical chunks. Paper presented at TALN 2006*. Leuven.
Wray, A. (2002). *Formulaic language and the lexicon*. Cambridge: Cambridge University Press.

Chapter 6
Collocation Candidate Extraction from Dependency-Annotated Corpora: Exploring Differences across Parsers and Dependency Annotation Schemes

Peter Uhrig, Stefan Evert, and Thomas Proisl

Abstract Collocation candidate extraction from dependency-annotated corpora has become more and more mainstream in collocation research over the past years. In most studies, however, the results of one parser are compared to those of relatively "dumb" window-based approaches only. To date, the impact of the parser used and its parsing scheme has not been studied systematically to the best of our knowledge. This chapter evaluates a total of 8 parsers on 2 corpora with 20 different association measures plus several frequency thresholds for 6 different types of collocations against the *Oxford Collocations Dictionary for Students of English* (2nd edition; 2009). We find that the parser and parsing scheme both play a role in the quality of the collocation candidate extraction. The performance of different parsers can differ substantially across different collocation types. The filters used to extract different types of collocations from the corpora also play an important role in the trade-off between precision and recall we can observe. Furthermore, we find that carefully sampled and balanced corpora (such as the BNC) seem to have considerable advantages in precision, but of course for total coverage, larger, less balanced corpora (such as the web corpus used in this study) take the lead. Overall, log-likelihood is the best association measure, but for some specific types of collocation (such as adjective-noun or verb-adverb), other measures perform even better.

P. Uhrig (✉) · S. Evert · T. Proisl
Friedrich-Alexander-Universität Erlangen-Nürnberg, Erlangen, Germany
e-mail: peter.uhrig@fau.de

P. Cantos-Gómez, M. Almela-Sánchez (eds.), *Lexical Collocation Analysis*, Quantitative Methods in the Humanities and Social Sciences,
https://doi.org/10.1007/978-3-319-92582-0_6

1 Introduction

While it is common practice to start a chapter on collocation candidate extraction with a lengthy discussion of the various concepts of collocation, we will keep this discourse to a minimum:[1] For the purpose of this paper, we define collocation as the combination of two lexical items as listed in collocations dictionaries, in our case in the *Oxford Collocations Dictionary for Students of English* (2nd edition; 2009). The rationale behind this is that the present paper aims to determine the best strategy to create lists of collocation candidates that can then be used in lexicography.

Evert (2004) identifies three approaches to the extraction of collocation candidates: segment-based co-occurrences, distance-based co-occurrences and relational co-occurrences. The segment-based approach relies on the statistical analysis of words that co-occur within some segment of text, e.g. a sentence or paragraph. The distance-based approach analyses words that co-occur within a short distance from each other that is usually defined as a window of orthographic words. Those two approaches require very little preprocessing and therefore were very popular when sufficiently fast and robust syntactic parsers were not readily available. The third approach, relational co-occurrences, analyses co-occurrences of words that are related by some (usually syntactic) relation. As such, it requires syntactically annotated corpora where the syntactic relation between words is made explicit. This requirement is met by dependency grammar. Studies have shown that relational co-occurrences are generally superior to segment-based or distance-based co-occurrences (cf. Uhrig and Proisl (2012), Bartsch and Evert (2014)).

However, a wide range of dependency parsers are available, and while there are many studies that have worked with such parsers to extract collocation candidates from corpora, their typical approach is to compare the results from one parser with distance-based or segment-based approaches. To date, no study we are aware of systematically compares different parsers against each other to determine the influence of the parser and/or its parsing scheme onto the quality of the extracted data. The present chapter tries to fill this gap.

2 Related Work

With the advent of sufficiently fast and accurate parsers, the extraction of collocation candidates based on syntactic relations, i.e. relational co-occurrences, has become one of the most popular approaches to collocation candidate extraction. All types of syntactic analysis have been used for collocation candidate extraction: partial or shallow syntactic analyses, phrase structure and dependency analyses.

[1] See Bartsch (2004: 27–39, 58–78) for a detailed overview.

Partial or shallow syntactic analyses have been used, for example, by Church et al. (1989), Basili et al. (1994), Kermes and Heid (2003) and Wermter and Hahn (2006). For several languages, the Sketch Engine (Kilgarriff et al. 2004) uses shallow analyses based on regular expressions over part-of-speech tags to define grammatical relations for word sketches. However, shallow parsing strategies have certain limitations. Ivanova et al. (2008), for example, find that for German the shallow approach is inferior to richer parsing strategies.

Phrase structure analyses have been used, for example, by Blaheta and Johnson (2001), Schulte im Walde (2003), Zinsmeister and Heid (2003, 2004), Villada Moirón (Villada and Begoña 2005), Seretan (2008) (cf. also Nerima et al. (2003), Seretan et al. (2003, 2004) and Seretan and Wehrli (2006)) and Sangati and van Cranenburgh (2015). It is worth noting that despite using a phrase structure parser, Seretan's extraction is based on grammatical relations between individual words, some of which are explicit in the parser's output, while others have to be inferred from the constituent structure.

Dependency analyses have been used, for example, by Teufel and Grefenstette (1995), Lin (1998, 1999), Pearce (2001), Lü and Zhou (2004), Heid et al. (2008), Weller and Heid (2010), Uhrig and Proisl (2012), Ambati et al. (2012) and Bartsch and Evert (2014).

Covarying collexeme analysis (Gries and Stefanowitsch 2004; Stefanowitsch and Gries 2005) is a minor extension of relational co-occurrences. Instead of analyzing words that are connected by a dependency relation, i.e. words that occur in two different slots in the same dependency relation, it analyses "words occurring in two different slots in the same construction" (Stefanowitsch and Gries 2009: 942). This means that covarying collexeme analysis introduces a slightly more general notion of co-occurrence: co-occurrence via a more complex syntactic structure instead of co-occurrence via a single dependency relation.

The conventional approach to collocation candidate extraction is to collect co-occurrence data and then rank candidate word pairs according to a measure of statistical association between the words. Such association measures compute a score from the co-occurrence frequency of the word pair and the marginal frequencies of the individual words, usually collected in the form of a 2×2 contingency table. A large number of association measures have been proposed in the literature. Evert (2004: 75–91) thoroughly discusses more than 30 different measures, Pecina (2005) gives a list of 84 measures, 57 of which are based on 2×2 contingency tables, and Wiechmann (2008: 253) compares 47 measures "in a task of predicting human behavior in an eye-tracking experiment". There is also a variety of approaches to the quantitative and qualitative evaluation of association measures for a given purpose, for example, Evert and Krenn (2001), Pearce (2002), Pecina (2005), Pecina and Schlesinger (2006), Wermter and Hahn (2006), Pecina (2010), Uhrig and Proisl (2012), Kilgarriff et al. (2014) and Evert et al. (2017).

Recent work has often focussed on the identification of particular types of lexicalized multiword expressions and complements association measures with other automatic methods for determining, for example, the compositionality (Katz and Giesbrecht 2006; Kiela and Clark 2013; Yazdani et al. 2015), non-modifiability

(Nissim and Zaninello 2013; Squillante 2014) or non-substitutability (Pearce 2001; Farahmand and Henderson 2016) of word combinations. There are also approaches that combine multiple sources of information with machine learning techniques (e.g. Tsvetkov and Wintner 2014). Finally, the approach taken by Rodríguez-Fernández et al. relies solely on distributional methods for a "semantics-driven recognition of collocations" (Rodríguez-Fernández et al. 2016: 499).

3 Methodology

3.1 *Corpora*

We evaluated the collocation candidate extraction from two very different corpora. The first is the *British National Corpus* (BNC) compiled in the early 1990s and comprising roughly 100 million words of running text. The BNC is carefully sampled to contain a wide range of text types, including 10 per cent spoken text. Since, by modern standards, the BNC cannot be counted among large corpora anymore, and since it is considerably older than the latest edition of the dictionary we use as gold standard (see Sect. 3.4), and since it is much smaller than what the compilers of the dictionary used, we decided to include ENCOW16A (Schäfer/Bildhauer Schäfer and Bildhauer 2012, Schäfer 2015), a corpus of English web pages comprising 16.8 billion tokens according to the official corpus documentation. Since we skipped all words that were recognized as so-called boilerplate (e.g. website navigation) by the COW team's software, the actual size of the corpus used in the present study is roughly 12.1 billion tokens.

3.2 *Models and Parsers*

For parsing to English phrase structure trees, there is only one basic standard, the Penn Treebank style (see Marcus et al. 1993). For English Dependencies, there exist different (often similar but not identical) styles, although much of the recent research seems to converge in the direction of Universal Dependencies (see Sect. 3.2.5 below). Since the decisions taken in the design of a dependency model are likely to influence the accuracy of collocation candidate extraction based on direct relations, we evaluate a set of five models, which are described briefly below together with the parsers that use them.

3.2.1 Combinatory Categorial Grammar (C&C)

The grammatical model used by C&C (Clark and Curran 2007)[2] is Combinatory Categorial Grammar (CCG; Steedman 2000). The dependency representation takes the form of predicate-argument structures with the predicate describing the relation and the governor and the dependent as arguments. However, C&C's output is the only one that incorporates additional arguments – besides governor and dependent – to cover extra information, for instance, on controlling verbs or on passives.

Thus, in example (1), we can observe that the third argument of the ncsubj predicate is empty ("_"). The dobj predicate only has two arguments.

(1) She considers the minister competent.

(ncsubj considered_1 She_0 _)
(dobj considered_1 minister_3)

In the output for (2) on the other hand, the third argument of the ncsubj predicate is "obj", indicating that while syntactically the element is a subject in this passive sentence, it corresponds to an object of the corresponding active sentence.

(2) The minister was considered competent.

(ncsubj considered_3 minister_1 obj)

For our purpose, grouping active clause object and passive clause subject together makes sense and is in line with the policy adopted by most lexicographers, e.g. in the V-N collocations presented by OCD2 (see Sect. 3.3 below for details). Thus we change the relation from ncsubj to obj in such cases in order to produce what we call "collapsed dependencies". Since the passive subject is ambiguous between direct and indirect object, we also collapse the relations dobj and obj2 to obj for consistency. While this processed C&C output is not fully "off-the-shelf", it has previously been used for collocation identification by Bartsch and Evert (2014) and Evert et al. (2017).

The parsing algorithm of C&C is a custom development "which maximizes the expected recall of dependencies" (Clark and Curran 2007: 495).

3.2.2 LTH (CoNLL 2009; Mate)

Johansson and Nugues (2007) created the dependency model that was used as the basis of the popular shared tasks at the CoNLL conferences from 2007 to 2009:

> "The new format was inspired by annotation practices used in other dependency treebanks with the intention to produce a better interface to further semantic processing than existing

[2]http://www.cl.cam.ac.uk/~sc609/candc-1.00.html

methods. In particular, we used a richer set of edge labels and introduced links to handle long-distance phenomena such as wh-movement and topicalization." (Johansson and Nugues 2007: 105).

In the meantime the CoNLL shared task has moved towards Universal Dependencies (see Sect. 3.2.5 below), but since mate-tools is not under very active development any more, with the main author working for Google on SyntaxNet now, it still uses the CoNLL 2009 format even in its latest version.

3.2.3 Stanford Typed Dependencies (Malt)

The Stanford Typed Dependencies format is described in detail by de Marneffe and Manning (2008). This also is a legacy format that has been superseded by Universal Dependencies (see Sect. 3.2.5 below), behind whose development it was certainly a driving force. Nonetheless, the Malt Parser with engmalt.linear-1.7 model that uses the projective stack algorithm described in Nivre (2009)[3] is used in this comparison, and the English language model is still based on a Penn Treebank version that makes use of Stanford Dependencies. It should be noted that Malt offers this model for "users who only want to have a decent robust dependency parser (and who are not interested in experimenting with different parsing algorithms, learning algorithms and feature models)"[4] because the focus of the Malt development is on implementing and comparing parsing algorithms – in its current version 1.9.1, it implements nine different algorithms.

3.2.4 CLEAR Style (nlp4j, spaCy)

Two parsers used here make use of the dependency representation called CLEAR style. The developers envisage it as a kind of synthesis of Stanford Dependencies and the (older) CoNLL style: "The dependency conversion described here takes the Stanford dependency approach as the core structure and integrates the CoNLL dependency approach to add long-distance dependencies, to enrich important relations like object predicates, and to minimize unclassified dependencies." (Choi and Palmer 2012: 6).

The dependency representation was created for ClearNLP (Choi and Palmer 2011; Choi and McCallum 2013) developed by Emory University's NLP group, which was the predecessor to NLP4J[5] 1.1.3 used in the present chapter. CLEAR style was later adopted by spaCy[6] for English, which we use in version 1.9.0 for this evaluation.

---

[3]http://www.maltparser.org/

[4]http://www.maltparser.org/mco/mco.html

[5]https://emorynlp.github.io/nlp4j/

[6]https://spacy.io/

While we would expect these parsers to produce comparable results, nlp4j does not follow the guidelines of the CLEAR style in the following example, while spaCy does:

(3) She is a competent minister.

Here, we would expect *competent* to be analysed as an adjectival modifier of *minister*, which is what spaCy does:

amod(minister, competent).

However, nlp4j consistently outputs the following relation:

nmod(minister, competent).

This is a nominal modifier, which is inconsistent with nlp4j's own PoS tagging, where *competent* is in fact tagged as an adjective. Parsing the entire BNC, nlp4j did not output a single amod relation. We will see in the evaluation below how this behaviour affects the collocation candidate extraction for noun-adjective collocations.

3.2.5 Universal Dependencies (Stanford, Stanford Converter [OpenNLP], SyntaxNet)

As hinted above, the Universal Dependencies[7] annotation scheme is on the point of becoming the standard for dependency parsing for any language:

> "The general philosophy is to provide a universal inventory of categories and guidelines to facilitate consistent annotation of similar constructions across languages, while allowing language-specific extensions when necessary." (http://universaldependencies.org/introduction.html).

In our comparison, the neural network dependency parser (Chen and Manning 2014) that is part of Stanford CoreNLP (Manning et al. 2014)[8] and Google's SyntaxNet with the Parsey McParseface model (Andor et al. 2016)[9] use Universal Dependencies, however in slightly different versions.[10] While SyntaxNet is limited to the standard "basic dependencies", Stanford's neural network parser can also produce "enhanced dependencies" and "enhanced++ dependencies" (Schuster and Manning 2016). The basic universal dependencies always form a tree (in the computer science sense of the word), i.e. each word is governed by exactly one other word unless it is the root of the sentence. The enhanced and enhanced++ representations "aim[...] to make implicit relations between content words more

[7] http://universaldependencies.org

[8] https://stanfordnlp.github.io/CoreNLP/

[9] https://github.com/tensorflow/models/tree/master/syntaxnet

[10] To date, the following revisions have been released: 1.0, 1.1, 1.2, 1.3, 1.4, 2.0

explicit by adding relations and augmenting relation names" (Schuster and Manning 2016: 2372). The additional relations may break the tree structure and the resulting analyses are (potentially cyclic) directed graphs.

Stanford CoreNLP and the Stanford Parser also include converters for converting a constituency analysis to a basic dependency analysis and for converting from basic dependencies to an enhanced and enhanced++ representation. We use only the former to convert the phrase structure analyses of Apache OpenNLP[11] to basic dependencies. This means that CoreNLP basic and Apache OpenNLP use exactly the same set of Universal Dependencies.

3.2.6 Summary

In sum we compare 11 combinations of parsers and models/postprocessing options in the present study, which are listed in Table 6.1.

3.3 *Gold Standard*

The gold standard used in the present study, i.e. the reference against which all parsers and models are compared, is the *Oxford Collocations Dictionary for Learners of English*, 2nd edition (OCD2 2009). It was compiled by lexicographers based on corpora consisting of "almost two billion words of text in English taken from up-to-date sources from around the world" (OCD2: vi). To our knowledge, the exact composition of the corpus collection has never been published, although we can assume that the BNC, which is the sole basis of the 1st edition of the dictionary

Table 6.1 Parsers and models/postprocessing options used in the present study

Parser	Model and postprocessing (if applicable)
C&C 1.00	Default
C&C 1.00	Collapsed
Stanford CoreNLP 3.8.0	Dependency neural network; basic dependencies
Stanford CoreNLP 3.8.0	Dependency neural network; enhanced dependencies
Stanford CoreNLP 3.8.0	Dependency neural network; enhanced++ dependencies
mate-tools 3.6.1	CoNLL2009-ST-English-ALL.anna-3.3
Malt 1.9.1	engmalt.linear-1.7.mco
NLP4J 1.1.3	Default
OpenNLP	Stanford CoreNLP 3.8.0 converter to basic dependencies
spaCy 1.9.0	en_core_web_sm
SyntaxNet 0.2 (April 2017)	Parsey McParseface

[11] https://opennlp.apache.org/

(2002), is included. In its microstructure, OCD2 distinguishes the different senses of the headword lemma, i.e. the base, where necessary and then uses "the grammatical construction as structural divisor" (Klotz and Herbst 2016: 228), i.e. it distinguishes the different types of collocations based on the word class and canonical order of base and collocate. The evaluation in this chapter takes into account the major types of collocations, which are listed in Table 6.1.

3.4 Processing Pipeline

The corpora were processed on FAU's high-performance computing systems to massively parallelize the time-consuming parsing process. After parsing, all instances of dependency relations were extracted together with the part-of-speech tags and lemmata of the governor and the dependent. If a parser supplied lemmata (CoreNLP, C&C, NLP4J, mate, Malt), these were used; if not (SyntaxNet, OpenNLP, spaCy), we applied the same rule-based English lemmatizer that was used in Uhrig and Proisl (2012). In order to ensure a fair evaluation against the OCD2 gold standard and to keep the amount of candidate data manageable, dependency pairs were matched against a word list of 42,720 lemmata, consisting of all headwords from the *Oxford Advanced Learner's Dictionary*, 8th edition (OALD8 2010), and all words that occur in OCD2 in one of the types of collocation listed in Table 6.2 (i.e. all headwords and all collocates). In order not to filter too aggressively, both the word form and the lemma of governor and dependent were compared to the word list; if either word form or lemma of both the governor and the dependent matched entries in the word list, the co-occurrence was accepted into the filtered dataset. For nouns, no difference between common nouns and proper nouns was made to include items such as *God* or various political institutions. However, most proper nouns were of course removed by the word list filter since neither dictionary contains many place names, personal names, or similar items.

Table 6.2 Overview of collocation types in our gold standard

Name in OCD	Abbreviation in this study	Pairs extracted from OCD2
[noun lemma] + verb	NVsubj	8979
verb + [noun lemma]	NVobj	36,670
[noun lemma] + adjective	NJ	86,379
[adjective lemma] + adverb	JV	7135
[verb lemma] + adjective	JR	11,625
[verb lemma] + adverb	VR	12,612

We extracted both unfiltered co-occurrence data (all dependency relations) and data filtered specifically for each collocation type.[12] Contingency tables were then compiled as described by Evert (2004: 33–37), using the UCS toolkit implementation.[13]

For the unfiltered data, lemmata were disambiguated by their part-of-speech category (noun, verb, adjective, adverb). We obtained between 9.2 and 17.1 million contingency tables (i.e. candidate lemma pairs) for the BNC and between 132.8 and 296.8 million contingency tables for ENCOW, depending on the parser and postprocessing used.

For the filtered data, we applied the restrictions listed in Table 6.3. We obtained between 24,148 and 1.6 million contingency tables for BNC, and between 274,492 and 20.6 million contingency tables for ENCOW, depending on syntactic relation[14] and parser.

We use the same set of 20 association measures for candidate ranking as Evert et al. (2017), which includes the most popular measures such as log-likelihood (G^2), t-score (t), z-score with Yates's correction (z), Mutual Information (MI), the Dice coefficient (which is used by the Sketch Engine) and ranking by co-occurrence frequency (f). In addition, we include different versions of the recently proposed ΔP measure (Gries 2013) and a conservative statistical estimate of MI ($\mathrm{MI}_{\mathrm{conf}}$; Johnson 1999). Since our focus here is on the comparison of different parsers, we refer to Evert et al. (2017) for a complete listing of the association measures with equations and references.

4 Evaluation

Following the evaluation methodology of Evert and Krenn (2001), we determine the quality of different n-best candidate lists for each candidate set and association ranking. Consider the example of the verb-object relation identified by the NLP4J parser in the BNC. Among the top 1,000 candidates ranked by log-likelihood, there are 801 true positives (TPs), i.e. actual collocations listed in OCD2. This 1,000-best list hence achieves a precision of 80.10%. However, the recall of this list is only 2.18% of the 36,670 object-verb collocations in OCD2. Similarly, a 10,000-best list achieves a precision of 66.50% and recall of 18.13% (with 6,650 TPs), and a 20,000-best list a precision of 56.16% and recall of 30.63% (with 11,232 TPs).

[12]Unfiltered data can be used to maximize recall, since parsers generally are better at predicting that two items should be connected by a dependency relation than they are at predicting what type of dependency relation connects the two. In the technical terms of parser evaluation, this is the difference between unlabelled and labelled attachment.

[13]http://www.collocations.de/software.html

[14]There are relatively few candidate pairs for verb-adjective and adverb-adjective collocations; the largest numbers of pairs are found for noun-verb (both subjects and objects) and noun-adjective collocations.

Table 6.3 Filters used for each type of collocation

Parser	Subj-V	V-Obj	Adj-N	V-Adj	V-Adv	Adv-Adj
C&C default	ncsubj(VB, NN)	dobj(VB, NN), obj2(VB, NN)	ncmod(NN, JJ)	xcomp(VB, JJ)	ncmod(VB, RB), dobj(VB, RB)	ncmod(JJ, RB)
C&C collapsed	subj(VB, NN)	obj(VB, NN)	ncmod(NN, JJ)	xcomp(VB, JJ)	ncmod(VB, RB), obj(VB, RB)	ncmod(JJ, RB)
CoreNLP basic	nsubj(VB, NN), nmod(VB, NN), acl(NN, VB)	dobj(VB, NN), nsubjpass(VB, NN)	amod(NN, JJ), nsubj(JJ, NN)	xcomp(VB, JJ), advcl(VB, JJ)	advmod(VB, RB)	advmod(JJ, RB)
CoreNLP basic v3 (see Sect. 3.2.5 for discussion)	nsubj(VB, NN)	dobj(VB, NN), nsubjpass(VB, NN)	amod(NN, JJ), nsubj(JJ, NN)	xcomp(VB, JJ), advcl(VB, JJ)	advmod(VB, RB)	advmod(JJ, RB)
CoreNLP enhanced	nsubj(VB, NN), nsubj:xsubj(VB, NN), nmod:agent(VB, NN)	dobj(VB, NN), nsubjpass(VB, NN)	amod(NN, JJ), nsubj(JJ, NN), nsubj:xsubj(JJ, NN)	xcomp(VB, JJ), advcl:as(VB, JJ)	advmod(VB, RB)	advmod(JJ, RB)
CoreNLP enhanced++	nsubj(VB, NN), nsubj:xsubj(VB, NN), nmod:agent(VB, NN)	dobj(VB, NN), nsubjpass(VB, NN)	amod(NN, JJ), nsubj(JJ, NN), nsubj:xsubj(JJ, NN)	xcomp(VB, JJ), advcl:as(VB, JJ)	advmod(VB, RB)	advmod(JJ, RB)
Mate	SBJ(VB, NN)	OBJ(VB, NN)	NMOD(NN, JJ)	PRD(VB, JJ), OPRD(VB, JJ)	ADV(VB, RB), OBJ(VB, RB), MNR(VB, RB), TMP(VB, RB)	AMOD(JJ, RB)
Malt	nsubj(VB, NN), infmod(NN, VB)	dobj(VB, NN), nsubjpass(VB, NN)	amod(NN, JJ), nsubj(JJ, NN)	acomp(VB, JJ), dep(VB, JJ)	advmod(VB, RB)	advmod(JJ, RB)

(continued)

Table 6.3 (continued)

Parser	Subj-V	V-Obj	Adj-N	V-Adj	V-Adv	Adv-Adj
NLP4J	nsubj(VB, NN)	dobj(VB, NN), nsubjpass(VB, NN)	nmod(NN, JJ), nsubj(JJ, NN)	acomp(VB, JJ), xcomp(VB, JJ)	advmod(VB, RB)	advmod(JJ, RB)
OpenNLP	nsubj(VB, NN), nmod(VB, NN)	dobj(VB, NN), nsubjpass(VB, NN)	amod(NN, JJ), nsubj(JJ, NN), compound(JJ, NN)	xcomp(VB, JJ), advcl(VB, JJ), amod(JJ, VB)	advmod(VB, RB)	advmod(JJ, RB)
spaCy	nsubj(VB, NN)	dobj(VB, NN), nsubjpass(VB, NN)	amod(NN, JJ), nsubj(JJ, NN)	acomp(VB, JJ), xcomp(VB, JJ)	advmod(VB, RB)	advmod(JJ, RB)
SyntaxNet	nsubj(VB, NN)	dobj(VB, NN), nsubjpass(VB, NN)	amod(NN, JJ), nsubj(JJ, NN)	acomp(VB, JJ), xcomp(VB, JJ)	advmod(VB, RB)	advmod(JJ, RB)

Each cell contains all relations used. Part-of-speech restrictions on governor and dependent are given in parentheses. The PoS tags used here are the first two letters of Penn Treebank tags to group various tags for the same word class (e.g. singular/plural for nouns) together

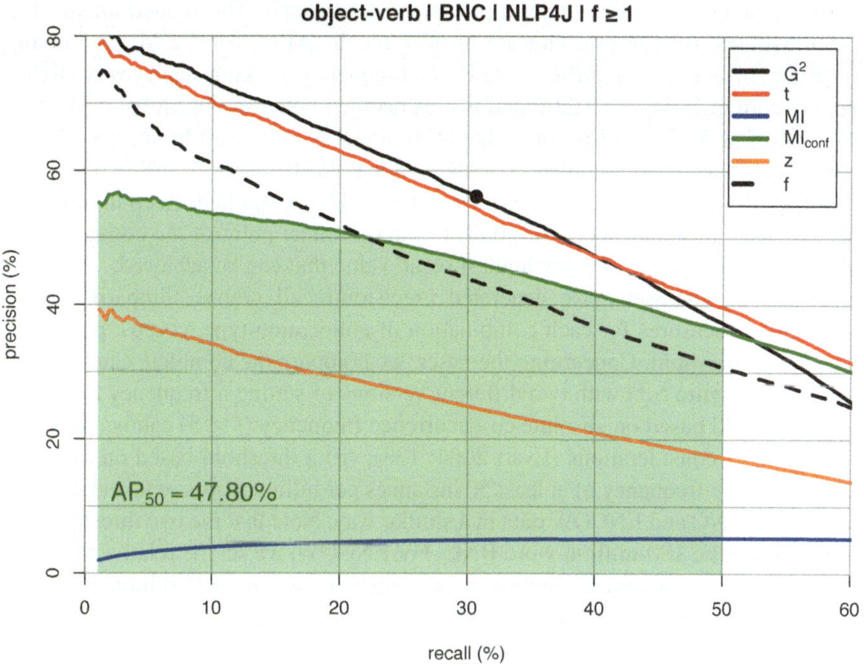

Fig. 6.1 Illustration of evaluation procedure using the methodology of Evert and Krenn (2001) and Evert et al. (2017). (Note that all our plots start at 2% recall since below this value the precision varies wildly and is not very meaningful)

Obviously, the size of an n-best list determines the trade-off between precision and recall. All possible n-best lists can be visualized at a single glance in the form of a precision-recall graph, shown as a solid black line in Fig. 6.1. The 20,000-best list above corresponds to a single point on this line marked by a small dot, at an x-coordinate of 30.63 and a y-coordinate of 56.16. Such precision-recall graphs allow for an easy comparison between different association measures. For example, it is obvious from Fig. 6.1 that log-likelihood (G^2) is a better choice than ranking by co occurrence frequency (f) because its precision values are always higher at the same recall percentage (mathematicians would say that G^2 is "uniformly better" than f). In turn, f is uniformly better than z-score (z), which is uniformly better than Mutual Information (MI).

Some other cases are less straightforward: G^2 is better than t-score (t) up to 40% recall but worse for higher recall percentages. MI_{conf} outperforms co-occurrence frequency for recall above 20% but achieves much lower precision in the front part of the graph. The choice of an optimal association measure thus depends on the recall required by an application. In order to make general comparisons of measures, parsers and other parameters, we need to define a composite evaluation criterion that summarizes the precision/recall graph in a single number. A customary approach is to compute the average of precision values at different recall points, corresponding to the area under a precision/recall graph. The shaded area in Fig. 6.1 illustrates average precision up to 50% recall (AP_{50}) for the MI_{conf} ranking, resulting in a score of $AP_{50} = 47.80\%$. Frequency ranking achieves a slightly better score of $AP_{50} = 49.22\%$ and is thus deemed better in our global evaluation. The cutoff at 50% recall is somewhat arbitrary. It is motivated by the fact that no candidate set achieves complete coverage of the gold standard (i.e. 100% recall) and coverage drops considerably if frequency thresholds are applied. Keep in mind that the coverage of a data set corresponds to the rightmost point of the corresponding precision/recall graphs, i.e. the highest recall value that can be achieved.

In the present study, we generated precision/recall graphs comparing all 20 association measures for each combination of collocation type, corpus, parser and frequency threshold. Concerning the latter, we compare the complete candidate set ($f \geq 1$, cf. Figure 6.1) with two different versions of setting a frequency threshold: (i) a threshold based on absolute co-occurrence frequency ($f \geq 5$) can be motivated by statistical considerations (Evert 2004: 133); (ii) a threshold based on a relative co-occurrence frequency of at least 50 instances per billion words of text ($f \geq 50/G$) affects the BNC and ENCOW data in a similar way. Note that the two thresholds are identical for the 100-million-word BNC. For ENCOW, we set the relative threshold at $f \geq 500$ co-occurrences, assuming a reduced effective size of 10 billion words that takes into account that our parsers extracted fewer instances of dependency relations from the same amount of text than for the BNC.

For each condition, we automatically determined the optimal association measure based on AP_{50} scores. These optimal results are used for global comparisons, but we also report more detailed findings from an inspection of the full precision/recall graphs. We also generated precision/recall graphs comparing different parsers (on the same collocation type, corpus and frequency threshold), using either the same association measure for all parsers or the optimal measure for each individual parser.

5 Results and Discussion

5.1 Association Measures

In order to keep the number of association measures manageable in the detailed discussion below, a selection had to be made from the full set of 20 association measures. As detailed in Sect. 4, for every combination of corpus (BNC, ENCOW16A), co-frequency threshold ($f \geq 1, f \geq 5, f \geq 50/G$), relation (subject-verb, verb-object, adjective-noun, verb-adjective, adjective-adverb, verb-adverb) and parser (see list in Table 6.1), the average precision at 50% recall (AP50) for every association measure was calculated, and the association measure with the highest AP50 was determined (i.e. if 50% recall was reached, which is not always the case when a frequency threshold is applied). Table 6.4 shows how often each association measure was

Table 6.4 Winning association measures at AP50 across relations

Assoc. Measure	NVsubj	NVobj	NJ	JV	JR	VR
log.likelihood	47	69	14	0	18	23
t.score	1	3	22	0	9	0
z.score.corr	12	0	0	0	0	0
frequency	0	0	0	38	0	0
MI4	0	0	0	4	0	0
MI.conf	2	0	0	0	9	36
DP.min	0	0	0	0	0	1

shown as the best measure broken down by relation. As we can see, only a few measures occur in the first position in one of the experiments. For the remainder of this chapter, we will only look at the most successful ones, i.e. frequency (which is of course not really an association measure and is only really relevant for verb-adjective collocations), log-likelihood, t-score and MI_{conf}.

There are some general observations which are true of all relations discussed in Sect. 5.2 and which are thus discussed in this section.

On the BNC, using a frequency threshold with MI_{conf} has a small positive effect. Overall, results without a frequency threshold are quite similar. On ENCOW, on the other hand, MI_{conf} without a frequency threshold performs poorly, which is probably due to the fact that ENCOW is several orders of magnitude larger than the BNC.

The extent to which a filter on dependency relations improves precision is dependent on the association measure in our dataset: The precision improves substantially for t-score and log-likelihood but much less so for MI_{conf}. We can illustrate this result with a comparison of the precision/recall curves for verb-adverb collocations in Fig. 6.2.

One further observation that is true of all relations is that the difference between Stanford CoreNLP with the enhanced and the enhanced++ models hardly results in visible differences in any of the graphs analysed, so the cover term *enhanced* will be used for both in the remainder of this chapter.

5.2 Comparison of Parsers by Collocation Type

To determine the performance of the parsers separately for each type of collocation, we analysed 16 graphs for each type, which were the result of combining the following factors: corpus (BNC, ENCOW16A), statistics (t-score, log-likelihood, MI_{conf}, frequency) and frequency threshold ($f \geq 1$ [i.e. no threshold], $f \geq 50/G$ [i.e. $f \geq 5$ for the BNC, $f \geq 500$ for ENCOW16A]). We will start with a detailed case study of subject-verb collocations to illustrate the analysis in detail. Since much of this is relevant to all types of collocation, the discussion of the remaining ones will be much less verbose.

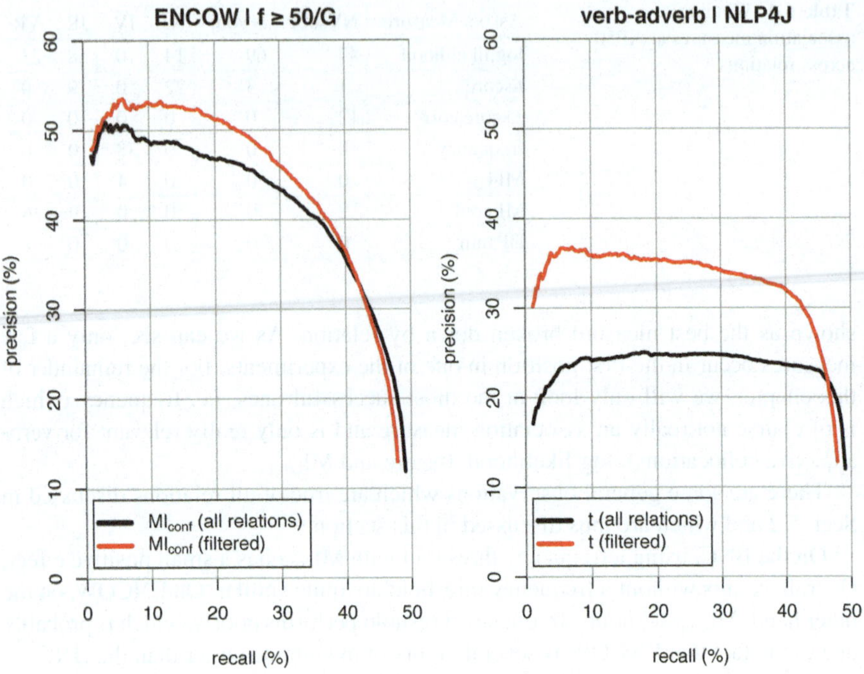

Fig. 6.2 Precision/recall curves for verb-adverb collocations in ENCOW16A with NLP4J

5.2.1 Subject-Verb

Examples:

(4) Her *boss hired* a new secretary.
(5) A new secretary was *hired* by her *boss*.
(6) Her boss wanted to *hire* a new *secretary*.
(7) Her colleague convinced her *boss* to *hire* a new secretary.
(8) Her *boss* had been convinced to *hire* a new secretary.
(9) Her colleague liked the new secretary *hired* by her *boss*.
(10) Her colleague liked the new secretary who had been *hired* by her *boss* the week before.

5.2.2 Overview

For the subject-verb collocations in the BNC, C&C, CoreNLP enhanced and NLP4J form the leading group in terms of precision. The latter only sees straightforward active clause subjects as in example (4) above, whereas C&C and CoreNLP enhanced also take by-agent phrases in the passive (example (5)) and subjects of non-finite subordinate clauses (example (6)) into account.

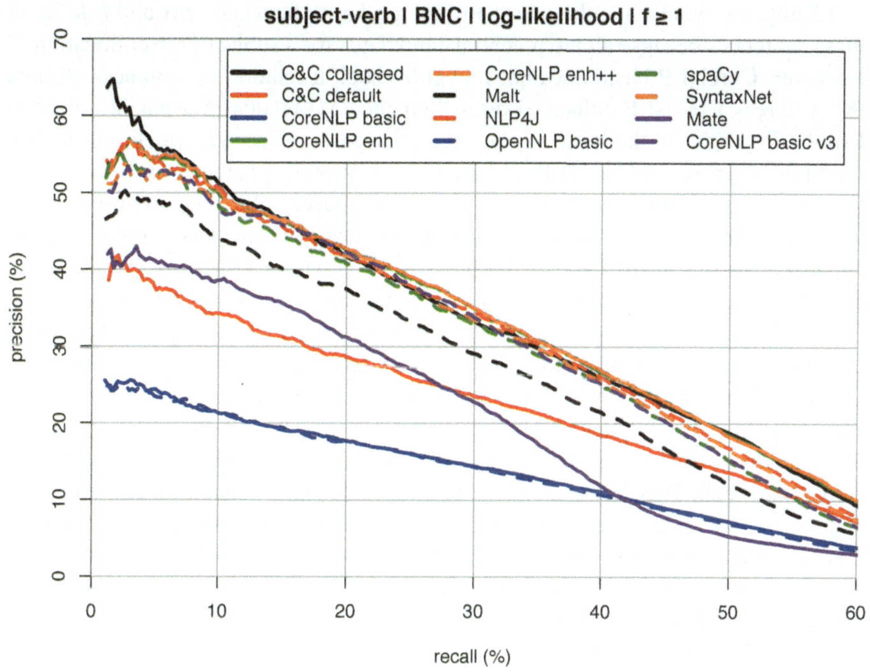

Fig. 6.3 Precision-recall graph for subject-verb collocation candidates from the BNC using log-likelihood and no frequency threshold

In ENCOW16A, CoreNLP basic v3 (see discussion below) performs best without a frequency threshold, but when a frequency threshold of 50/G is applied, recall and precision at above 30% recall are reduced compared to CoreNLP enhanced and C&C, precisely because the latter also include cases such as examples (2) and (3). Surprisingly, mate performs much worse than CoreNLP basic v3, even though it should also show this high precision according to the parsing model. Since precision is generally very low for subject-verb collocations in our experiments on ENCOW16A, a more thorough investigation follows below.

5.2.3 Detailed Discussion

In Fig. 6.3 we can observe that the precision up to 50% recall is very bad for the collocation candidate extraction labelled "Core NLP basic" and very good for the version labelled "CoreNLP basic (v3)". Both lines in the graph are based on the same output from Stanford CoreNLP, but the collocation candidate extraction is different. This can be explained if we take a look at how CoreNLP processes the example sentences (4) to (10).

Ideally, we would like the parser to find a relation between *boss* and *hire* in all these sentences because all are potential candidates for a subject-verb collocation.[15] However, CoreNLP basic does not recognize such a relation in sentences (6) and (8), whereas CoreNLP enhanced does. Sentence (7) results in a parsing error in CoreNLP, where, in the basic variant, the relation is called acl, which is a clausal modifier of a noun. In CoreNLP enhanced, the relation is specified as acl:to, because the enhanced variant adds the element called "marker" (i.e. the subordinator or infinitive marker) to the relation name. CoreNLP basic is also less explicit than the enhanced variant in the case of the passive *by*-agents in sentences (5), (9), (10), for which the very general nmod (nominal modifier) relation is used, while the enhanced variant uses nmod:agent for (5) and (10) and nmod:by for (9), which probably should also be nmod:agent instead and may thus be due to an error in the conversion rules from basic to enhanced dependencies. In our first run of the collocation candidate extraction, we decided to include both nmod and acl in the extraction rules for subject-verb collocations for CoreNLP basic in order to maximize recall. This, however, led to the extremely bad precision we can witness in Fig. 6.3 (and which is very similar to that of OpenNLP since we also use CoreNLP basic dependencies for it). The curve labelled "CoreNLP basic v3" is geared towards high precision by removing both nmod and acl in the list of possible relations for subject-verb collocations. The curves for CoreNLP enhanced/enhanced++ contain both acl:to and nmod:agent.

For C&C, there is a similar issue in that C&C default does not distinguish between active-clause subjects and passive-clause subjects, which considerably reduces its precision. C&C collapsed, which makes the distinction, is among the top parsers.

Of course, CoreNLP basic v3, SyntaxNet and the other parsers that are at the top of the graphs for some of the association scores might achieve better precisions by sacrificing recall, which cannot be seen from our evaluation plots (up to 50% recall).[16] However, the information is available in the coverage overview plots.

As we can see in Fig. 6.4, the choice really is a trade-off between precision and recall in that CoreNLP basic with all relations finds considerably more relevant items ("true positives") than CoreNLP basic v3, but at the cost of including a very high number of irrelevant items ("false positives"). When the corpus is large enough and the frequency threshold is relatively low, the differences in coverage are much smaller and high precision becomes the major criterion for the performance of a parser for collocation candidate extraction.

One more observation we can gather from comparing different plots for subject-verb collocation candidates is that precision is on an average level for the BNC (AP50 ~38.5%) but relatively low for ENCOW16A (AP50 ~22.5%). This is not an issue of gold standard collocations missing from the corpus, though. Without

[15]That is, of course, if the definition of the collocation type is regarded as a lexical phenomenon with the terminology based on the canonical active-declarative structure.

[16]Except for graphs where the high frequency threshold leads to a coverage of less than 50%

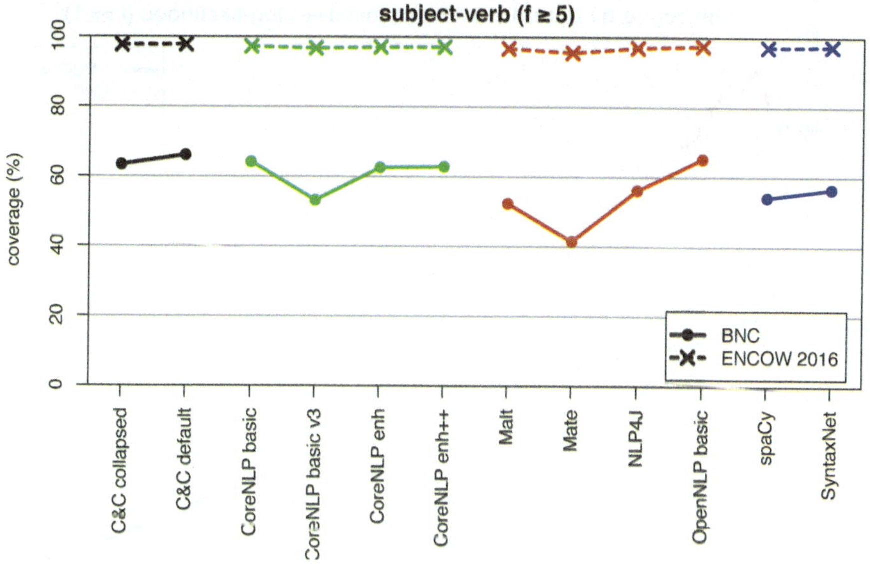

Fig. 6.4 Coverage of subject-verb collocation candidates for BNC and ENCOW 2016 with $f \geq 5$

frequency threshold, coverage is 89.9% for the BNC and 97.9% for ENCOW. For a closer look, we focus on log-likelihood, which achieves good AP50 across both corpora regardless of frequency threshold (justifying coverage without threshold), even though $\mathrm{MI}_{\mathrm{conf}}$ is slightly better on the BNC with $f \geq 5$ (but extremely bad on ENCOW). The plot below shows the full precision-recall curves of log-likelihood (Fig. 6.5):

Thus the problem lies clearly not in a lack of coverage, but in the ranking of candidates, particularly in the case of ENCOW16A. One observation is that coverage is affected very much by frequency threshold, dropping to a bit over 60% (BNC, $f \geq 5$) or even below 50% (ENCOW, $f \geq 50/G$), which suggests that one problem may be that many subject-verb collocations are very infrequent in the two corpora.

In order to determine why ENCOW16A is so much worse than the BNC, the first 1,000 collocation candidates from ENCOW16A (corresponding to a recall of up to 3.17%) and from the BNC (corresponding to a recall of up to 5.81%) were exported for manual inspection for two parsers, CoreNLP enhanced++ and SyntaxNet. Both files overlap, so in total 1,592 pairs were collected for CoreNLP and 1,577 pairs for SyntaxNet. The first 1,000 items from the BNC contain 551 true positives, i.e. items present in the gold standard, for CoreNLP and 522 for SyntaxNet, whereas the first 1,000 items from ENCOW16A only contain 283 true positives for CoreNLP and 285 for SyntaxNet.

The most important reason for the striking difference between the two corpora seems to be repeated usage in ENCOW16A, where the same text appears on many webpages. Often this is boilerplate, as in the following examples:

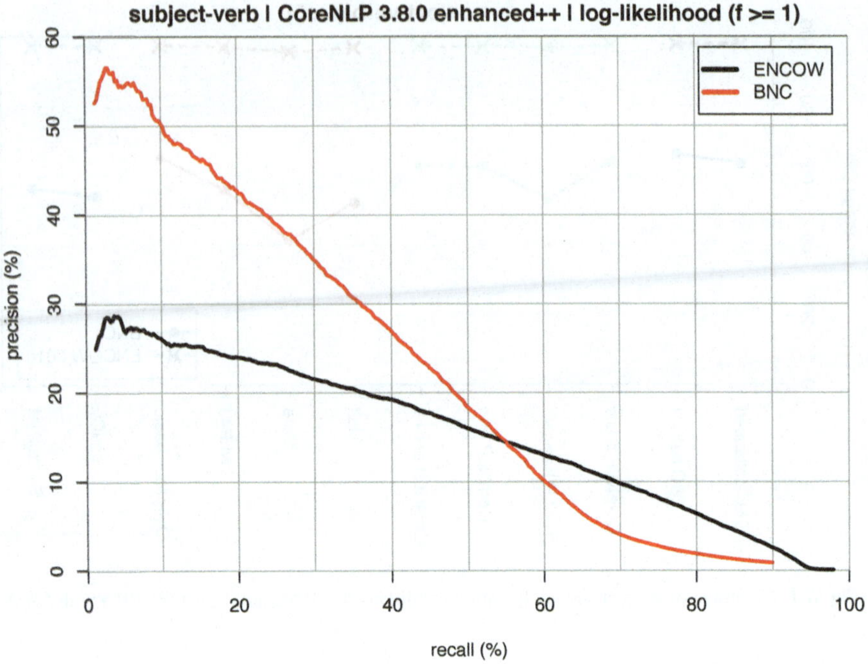

Fig. 6.5 Precision/recall curves for subject-verb collocations with CoreNLP enhanced++, log-likelihood and without a frequency threshold

(11) Grapeshot stores the categories of story you have been exposed to. (>200,000)
(12) Failure to return items with all the required documentation will result in a delay in processing the return and may even invalidate the return itself. (>20,000)
(13) People also look for caravans to rent, apple 3 g iphone, small holdings to rent, top online classifieds for pets in England, laptop computers, bedsits in london, free world ads and many more interesting items. (>26,000)

Sentence (11) can be found on many different websites because Grapeshot is an online marketing company. Sentence (12) is from the return policy of an online shoe store from which more than 20,000 product pages found their way into the corpus. Sentence (13) appears to be search-engine spam, i.e. a set of many webpages whose only purpose is to appear at the top of the search results for many search terms and earn money through ads. With such high frequencies, it is of course not surprising that the combination of *Grapeshot* + *store* takes the second-highest position of all collocation candidates in ENCOW16A for SyntaxNet.[17] Some more such candidates in the top 1,000 in ENCOW16A are *type* + *visit*,

[17] CoreNLP produces a parsing error on this sentence so that *Grapeshot stores* is wrongly analysed as a nominal compound.

widget + *give*, *site* + *function*, *website* + *use*, *site* + *set*, *cookie* + *store*, *list* + *update*, *story* + *match*, *delivery* + *take*, *site* + *use* and *feature* + *require*.

There is one further problem of repeated usage: If the parser produces an error in the parse for this particular sentence, it will do the same in all repeated instances. In sentence (13), *caravan* should be analysed as object of *rent* and thus should not occur in the list in the first place, but it is in fact treated as subject of *rent* by both parsers. This problem is particularly pronounced in sentence fragments with past participles, where the parser often identifies the participle as past tense verb and thus the object in front of it as subject:

(14) All rights reserved. (error only in SyntaxNet)
(15) No pun intended / Pun intended. (error in both parsers)

The combination of *right* + *reserve* is the top subject-verb collocation candidate for ENCOW16A in our list for SyntaxNet, and again it is due to a parsing error combined with completely skewed frequencies.

There are more such cases of repeated fragments, which can be part of completely different texts. For instance, the combination *allah* + *bless* occurs frequently, since it is due to the conventionalized complimentary phrase given in (16), which is attached to the names of prophets in Islam.

(16) may Allah bless him and grant him peace

The combination occurs almost 18,000 times, with the bulk of these hits coming from one website on Islamic topics (bewley.virtualave.net), which, according to its start page, provides mainly transcripts of talks and translations of texts from Arabic. Still, the phrase is added to every occurrence of *Mohammed* or *Messenger of Allah*, so it is no real boilerplate but just convention.[18]

ENCOW16A is of course also skewed in many other respects. As expected in a web corpus, there is some language related to computer technology or innovations that are relevant for computers, although the vocabulary filter will already have eliminated many of these. Examples are *cursor* + *hover*, *screen* + *freeze*, *blog* + *cover* and *administrator* + *accept*.

Furthermore, it is likely that our gold standard, OCD2, is biased towards British English, so collocation candidates from other varieties (in particular US-American English) will also influence the precision negatively, e.g. *congress* + *enact*.

Let us now turn to the reasons why we are still far from 100% precision at the top of the collocation candidate list, even in the BNC.

One reason is the number of co-occurrences with the verb *be*. Out of the 1,592 (CoreNLP enhanced++)/1,577 (SyntaxNet) items in the combined top 1,000 list from ENCOW16A and the BNC, there are 128/162 candidates with the verb *be*, 124/155 of which (113/131 from the BNC, 97/117 from ENCOW16A) are false positives, i.e. are not listed in OCD2. The top 10 of the list from ENCOW16A

[18]The same is true of the alternative form "peace be upon him", which occurs more than 10,000 times but does not propel *peace* + *be* into the to 1,000 collocation candidates.

comprises *way*, *reason*, *problem*, *thing*, *point*, *question*, *aim*, *purpose*, *goal* and *suggestion*. Except for *goal*, these are all quite strong in the BNC, too. It is clear that even if such items co-occur relatively frequently with *be*, it is questionable whether they should be listed in a collocations dictionary. Still, some are of course similar in fixedness and frequency to the seven true positives[19] in the lists, *cause*, *difference*, *focus*, *issue*, *secret*, *time* and *truth*, so what it is that made the lexicographers include them in OCD2 but not *reason*, *problem* or *point* remains an open question.

Another large proportion of false positives are unspecific combinations. Some of these occur with general (pro)nouns, e.g. *anyone* + *know*, *someone* + *tell* or *people* + *want*, but many are just common words occurring more frequently than expected based on their individual frequencies, such as *company* + *pay*, *group* + *meet*, *school* + *have* or *wife* + *die*, a fact that is "neither particularly surprising nor particularly interesting" (Herbst 1996: 382), just like the example of *sell* + *house* quoted by Herbst.

Finally, there are cases that may just as well figure in a collocations dictionary, for instance, *section* + *describe*, *government* + *propose* or *budget* + *grow*, but that are not part of our gold standard.

A complementary perspective is offered by examining true positives (TPs) from the gold standard with particularly low log-likelihood scores. The 1,000 TPs with lowest G^2 scores in ENCOW16A were thus also subjected to closer scrutiny. The histogram in Fig. 6.6 shows that their low rank is not an issue of data sparseness: most of the candidates have $f \geq 10$, a substantial portion even $f \geq 100$; but a considerable number of high-frequency pairs occur *less often than expected* in ENCOW16A.

In the list, we find some problematic items, where the gold standard is slightly dubious, e.g. *evidence* + *grow*, which is not impossible but rare compared to the much more common *growing evidence*, where it would be problematic to say that *evidence* is the subject of the verb *grow*.

Many of the low-ranked pairs contain frequent general-purpose verbs (*be*, *go*, *come*, *say*) and relatively frequent nouns (*website*, *problem*, *company*, *system*). Sometimes, skewage in the corpus may be responsible for the low values, for instance, the word *website* occurs roughly 200,000 times with the verb *adhere* and roughly 250,000 times with the verb *use* in the top 1,000 list. This means of course that the expected frequency of the combination *website* + *be* goes up to unnaturally high levels, so that it occurs less frequently than expected (roughly 29,000 hits).

Some of the items are listed with extremely low frequencies, which may be due to parsing/tagging errors. This is particularly obvious in examples such as *tiger* + *spring* or *duck* + *nest*, where the verb was often analysed as a noun by the parsers.

[19] The list for CoreNLP enhanced++ only contains four of them.

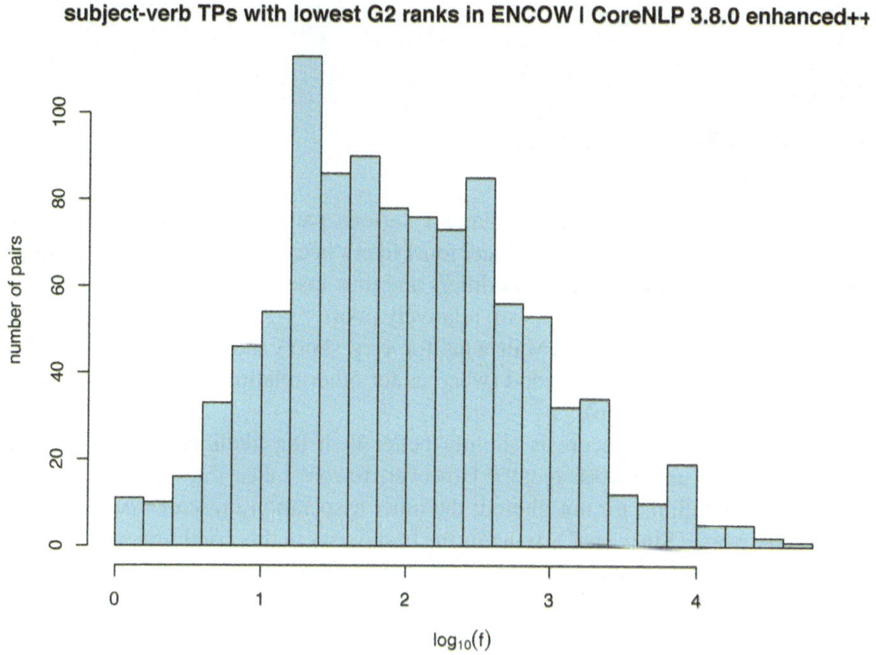

Fig. 6.6 Histogram of the 1,000 lowest-ranked true positive subject-verb collocations on ENCOW16A with CoreNLP enhanced++

5.3 Verb-Object

Examples:

(17) She won the match.
(18) The first *match* was *won* by the Dutch champion.

Overall, the differences between the various parsers are small when it comes to verb-object collocations. The best performance is offered by spaCy and nlp4j, the worst by C&C. Surprisingly, C&C collapsed dependencies are usually slightly worse than the default model used by C&C.

In terms of association measures, we can observe that log-likelihood is slightly better than t-score on the BNC. These differences disappear in ENCOW16A. MI_{conf} is substantially worse than log-likelihood and t-score, particularly for short candidate lists; however, MI_{conf}'s performance improves significantly with the application of a frequency threshold in ENCOW, even though it never reaches the performance of log-likelihood or t-score.

5.4 Adjective-Noun

Examples:

(19) Her boyfriend is really handsome.
(20) He is a very *handsome man*.

Again, the results are very similar for various parsers. Here spaCy wins, but nlp4j does not perform above average, most likely because it does not differentiate between adjectival and nominal modifiers and thus loses precision offered by most other parsers. CoreNLP's results are relatively poor.

On the BNC with t-score, Malt wins for very short candidate lists (up to 10% recall) and is generally quite good (whereas for other relations, it is usually part of the low-performing group).

For ENCOW16A, t-score is slightly better than log-likelihood for very short candidate lists (up to 10% recall). However, t-score takes the biggest hit when dependency relations are not filtered; the other association measures perform only minimally worse. Since spaCy remains the best parser in this condition, we can state that it seems to be excellent both at labelled and unlabelled attachment.

5.5 Verb-Adjective

Examples:

(21) This sounds ingenious.
(22) He pleaded innocent.

Overall, there is very little data for this type of collocation simply because it is comparatively rare. We can observe very high precision, which may indicate that there is only limited variability in both slots. Verb-adjective collocations are the only ones for which simple co-occurrence frequency performs better than any of the association measures. MI_{conf}'s statistics seem to be particularly bad for this type of construction.

In terms of parsers, C&C and mate-tools win. On ENCOW16A nlp4j performs best for short candidate lists.

5.6 Verb-Adverb

Example:

(23) He brutally assaulted her.

The best-performing parser are spaCy, nlp4j and CoreNLP, but generally there is little difference between the parsers, except for mate and C&C, both of which deliver a recall value of almost 10 percentage points below that of other parsers. For the BNC, the frequency threshold does not make much of a difference, but for ENCOW16A, the image is reversed: Without the frequency threshold, MI_{conf} performs worst among the association measures; with a frequency threshold of 50/G, MI_{conf} performs best. Log-likelihood outperforms t-score in both conditions.

Interestingly, C&C becomes the best parser (though still with a slightly lower recall than most others) when dependency relations are not filtered, which suggests that the labelled attachment causes trouble here.

5.7 Adverb-Adjective

Example:

(24) He is a *highly capable* manager.

We can observe that Malt is generally bad for this type of collocation. OpenNLP with Stanford Converter, CoreNLP and SyntaxNet are fairly close to one another in their results and usually perform neither particularly well nor particularly badly. The best parsers are spaCy, nlp4j and C&C.

Again, log-likelihood performs best in most conditions and is only outperformed by MI_{conf} for short candidate lists with a high frequency threshold of 50/G on ENCOW16A.

6 Conclusion

In this chapter, we have shown that there are no simple solutions for the best possible way to extract collocation candidates. Nonetheless, we can recommend certain practices over others on the basis of our research. Overall, spaCy is a robust parser with good results on all relations. On some specific relations (e.g. subject-verb), it is outperformed by other parsers, but there is no relation where spaCy shows a real weakness. Usually it is part of the leading group in the graph, and it achieves most often the best average precision at 50% recall (AP50).

As for the association measures, we can say that overall log-likelihood is an association measure that works well on all relations even though for some types of collocations, other measures surpass it, e.g. t-score for adjective-noun, MI_{conf} for verb-adverb or co-occurrence frequency for verb-adjective. Thus for general-purpose collocation research, we can recommend log-likelihood. For maximum precision for particular relations, for instance, in software used for lexicographic purposes, it would be beneficial to select different association measures for the different relations.

References

Ambati, B. R., Reddy, S., & Kilgarriff, A. (2012). Word sketches for Turkish. In N. Calzolari, K. Choukri, T. Declerck, M. U. Doğan, B. Maegaard, J. Mariani, A. Moreno, J. Odijk, & S. Piperidis (Eds.), *Proceedings of the eighth international conference on language resources and evaluation (LREC'12)* (pp. 2945–2950). Istanbul: European Language Resources Association http://www.lrec-conf.org/proceedings/lrec2012/pdf/585_Paper.pdf.

Andor, D., Alberti, C., Weiss, D., Severyn, A., Presta, A., Ganchev, K., Petrov, S., & Collins, M. (2016). Globally normalized transition-based neural networks. In *Proceedings of the 54th annual meeting of the Association for Computational Linguistics (ACL'16)* (pp. 2442–2452). Berlin: Association for Computational Linguistics http://aclweb.org/anthology/P16-1231.

Bartsch, S. (2004). *Structural and functional properties of collocations in English. A corpus study of lexical and pragmatic constraints on lexical co-occurrence*. Tübingen: Narr.

Bartsch, S., & Evert, S. (2014). Towards a Firthian notion of collocation. *OPAL – Online publizierte Arbeiten zur Linguistik, 2*(2014), 48–61 http://pub.ids-mannheim.de/laufend/opal/pdf/opal2014-2.pdf.

Basili, R., Pazienza, M. T., & Velardi, P. (1994). A 'not-so-shallow' parser for collocational analysis. In *Proceedings of the 15th conference on computational linguistics (COLING'94)* (pp. 447–453). Tokyo: Association for Computational Linguistics http://aclweb.org/anthology/C94-1074.

Blaheta, D., & Johnson, M. (2001). Unsupervised learning of multi-word verbs. In *Proceedings of the ACL workshop on collocation: Computational extraction, analysis and exploitation* (pp. 54–60). Toulouse.: http://web.science.mq.edu.au/~mjohnson/papers/2001/dpb-colloc01.pdf.

Chen, D., & Manning, C. D. (2014). A fast and accurate dependency parser using neural networks. In A. Moschitti, B. Pang, & W. Daelemans (Eds.), *Proceedings of the 2014 conference on empirical methods in natural language processing (EMNLP'14)* (pp. 740–750). Doha: Association for Computational Linguistics http://aclweb.org/anthology/D14-1082.

Choi, J. D., & McCallum, A. (2013). Transition-based dependency parsing with Selectional branching. In *Proceedings of the 51st annual meeting of the Association for Computational Linguistics (ACL'13)* (pp. 1052–1062). Sofia: Association for Computational Linguistics http://aclweb.org/anthology/P13-1104.

Choi, J. D., & Palmer, M. (2011). Getting the most out of transition-based dependency parsing. In *Proceedings of the 49th annual meeting of the Association for Computational Linguistics: Human language technologies (ACL'11)* (pp. 687–692). Portland: Association for Computational Linguistics http://aclweb.org/anthology/P11-2121.

Choi, J. D., & Palmer, M. (2012). *Guidelines for the CLEARStyle Constituent to Dependency Conversion*. Institute of Cognitive Science Technical Report 01-12, University of Colorado Boulder.

Church, K., Gale, W., Hanks, P., & Hindle, D. (1989). Parsing, word associations and typical predicate-argument relations. In *Speech and natural language: Proceedings of a workshop held at cape cod, Massachusetts, October 15-18, 1989* (pp. 75–81). Cape Cod.: http://aclweb.org/anthology/H89-2012.

Clark, S., & Curran, J. R. (2007). Wide-coverage efficient statistical parsing with CCG and log-linear models. *Computational Linguistics, 33*(4), 493–556 http://aclweb.org/anthology/J07-4004.

Evert, S. (2004). *The statistics of word Cooccurrences. Word pairs and collocations*. Ph.D. thesis, Institut für maschinelle Sprachverarbeitung, Universität Stuttgart. Published in 2005 http://elib.uni-stuttgart.de/opus/volltexte/2005/2371/.

Evert, S., & Krenn, B. (2001). Methods for the qualitative evaluation of lexical association measures. In *Proceedings of the 39th annual meeting of the Association for Computational Linguistics (ACL'01)* (pp. 188–195). Toulouse: Association for Computational Linguistics http://www.aclweb.org/anthology/P01-1025.

Evert, S., Uhrig, P., Bartsch, S., & Proisl, T. (2017). E-VIEW-alation – A large-scale evaluation study of association measures for collocation identification. In *Proceedings of eLex 2017 – Electronic lexicography in the 21st century: Lexicography from Scratch* (pp. 531–549). Leiden: Lexical Computing https://elex.link/elex2017/wp-content/uploads/2017/09/paper32.pdf.

Farahmand, M., & Henderson, J. (2016). Modeling the non-substitutability of multiword expressions with distributional semantics and a log-linear model. In *Proceedings of the 12th workshop on multiword expressions* (pp. 61–66). Berlin: Association for Computational Linguistics https://aclweb.org/anthology/W16-1809.

Gries, S. T. (2013). 50-something years of work on collocations: What is or should be next .... *International Journal of Corpus Linguistics, 18*(1), 137–165.

Gries, S. T., & Stefanowitsch, A. (2004). Covarying collexemes in the into-causative. In M. Achard & S. Kemmer (Eds.), *Language, culture, and mind* (pp. 225–236). Stanford, CA: CSLI.

Heid, U., Fritzinger, F., Hauptmann, S., Weidenkaff, J., Weller, M. (2008). Providing corpus data for a dictionary for German juridical phraseology. In Storrer, A., Geyken, A., Siebert, A., Würzner, K-M, Text resources and lexical knowledge. Selected papers from the 9th conference on natural language processing, KONVENS 2008, Berlin, Germany (pp. 131–144). Berlin/Boston: Mouton de Gruyter. https://doi.org/10.1515/9783110211818.2.131

Herbst, T. (1996). What are collocations: Sandy beaches or false teeth? In *English studies* (Vol. 1996/4, pp. 379–393).

Ivanova, K., Heid, U., Walde, S. S. i., Kilgarriff, A., & Pomikalek, J. (2008). Evaluating a German sketch grammar: A case study on noun phrase case. In N. Calzolari, K. Choukri, B. Maegaard, J. Mariani, J. Odijk, S. Piperidis, & D. Tapias (Eds.), *Proceedings of the sixth international conference on language resources and evaluation (LREC'08)*. Marrakech: European Language Resources Association, 2101–2107 http://www.lrec-conf.org/proceedings/lrec2008/pdf/537_paper.pdf.

Johansson, R., & Nugues, P. (2007). Extended constituent-to-dependency conversion for English. In *Proceedings of NODALIDA 2007* (pp. 105–112). Tartu.: http://dspace.ut.ee/bitstream/handle/10062/2560/reg-Johansson-10.pdf.

Johnson, M. (1999). *Confidence intervals on likelihood estimates for estimating association strengths*. Unpublished technical report.

Katz, G., & Giesbrecht, E. (2006). Automatic identification of non-compositional multi-word expressions using latent semantic analysis. In *Proceedings of the workshop on multiword expressions: Identifying and exploiting underlying properties (MWE'06)* (pp. 12–19). Sydney: Association for Computational Linguistics http://aclweb.org/anthology/W06-1203.

Kermes, H., & Heid, U. (2003). Using chunked corpora for the acquisition of collocations and idiomatic expressions. In F. Kiefer & J. Pajzs (Eds.), *Proceedings of 7th conference on computational lexicography and Corpus research*. Budapest: Research Institute for Linguistics, Hungarian Academy of Sciences.

Kiela, D., & Clark, S. (2013). Detecting compositionality of multi-word expressions using nearest neighbours in vector space models. In *Proceedings of the 2013 conference on empirical methods in natural language processing (EMNLP'13)* (pp. 1427–1432). Seattle: Association for Computational Linguistics http://www.aclweb.org/anthology/D13-1147.

Kilgarriff, A., Rychlý, P., Smrz, P., & Tugwell, D. (2004). The sketch engine. In G. Williams & S. Vessier (Eds.), *Proceedings of the 11th EURALEX international congress* (pp. 105–115). Lorient: Université de Bretagne Sud, Faculté des lettres et des sciences humaines http://euralex.org/wp-content/themes/euralex/proceedings/Euralex%202004/011_2004_V1_Adam%20KILGARRIFF,%20Pavel%20RYCHLY,%20Pavel%20SMRZ,%20David%20TUGWELL_The%20%20Sketch%20Engine.pdf.

Kilgarriff, A., Rychlý, P., Jakubicek, M., Kovář, V., Baisa, V., & Kocincová, L. (2014). Extrinsic corpus evaluation with a collocation dictionary task. In N. Calzolari, K. Choukri, T. Declerck, H. Loftsson, B. Maegaard, J. Mariani, A. Moreno, J. Odijk, & S. Piperidis (Eds.), *Proceedings of the ninth international conference on language resources and evaluation (LREC'14)*. Reykjavik: European Language Resources Association http://www.lrec-conf.org/proceedings/lrec2014/pdf/52_Paper.pdf.

Klotz, M., & Herbst, T. (2016). *English dictionaries: A linguistic introduction*. Berlin: Erich Schmidt.

Lin, D. (1998). Extracting collocations from text corpora. In *Proceedings of the first workshop on computational terminology* (pp. 57–63). Montreal.

Lin, D. (1999). Automatic identification of non-compositional phrases. In *Proceedings of the 37th annual meeting of the Association for Computational Linguistics (ACL'99)* (pp. 317–324). Morristown: Association for Computational Linguistics http://aclweb.org/anthology/P99-1041.

Lü, Y., & Zhou, M. (2004). Collocation translation acquisition using monolingual corpora. In *Proceedings of the 42nd meeting of the Association for Computational Linguistics (ACL'04)* (pp. 167–174). Barcelona: Association for Computational Linguistics http://aclweb.org/anthology/P04-1022.

Manning, C. D., Surdeanu, M., Bauer, J., Finkel, J. R., Bethard, S., & McClosky, D. (2014). The Stanford CoreNLP natural language processing toolkit. In *Proceedings of the 52nd annual meeting of the Association for Computational Linguistics (ACL'14)* (pp. 55–60). Baltimore: Association for Computational Linguistics http://aclweb.org/anthology/P14-5010.

Marcus, M. P., Marcinkiewicz, M. A., & Santorini, B. (1993). Building a large annotated corpus of English: The Penn Treebank. *Computational Linguistics, 19*(2), 313–330 http://aclweb.org/anthology/J93-2004.

Marneffe, M.-C. de & Manning, C. D. (2008). Stanford dependencies manual. https://nlp.stanford.edu/software/dependencies_manual.pd

Nerima, L., Seretan, V., & Wehrli, E. (2003). Creating a multilingual collocations dictionary from large text corpora. In *Companion volume to the proceedings of the 10th conference of the European chapter of the Association for Computational Linguistics (EACL'03)* (pp. 131–134). Budapest: Association for Computational Linguistics http://aclweb.org/anthology/E03-1022.

Nissim, Malvina, Andrea Zaninello (2013): "Modeling the internal variability of multi-word expressions through a pattern-based method." *ACM Transactions on Speech and Language Processing (TSLP)* 10/2: 7:1–7:26. https://doi.org/10.1145/2483691.2483696

Nivre, J. (2009). Non-projective dependency parsing in expected linear time. In *Proceedings of the 47th annual meeting of the Association for Computational Linguistics and the 4th international joint conference on natural language processing of the AFNLP (ACL'09)* (pp. 351–359). Singapore: Association for Computational Linguistics http://www.aclweb.org/anthology/P09-1040.

Pearce, D. (2001). Synonymy in collocation extraction. In *Proceedings of the NAACL workshop on WordNet and other lexical resources: Applications, extensions and customizations* (pp. 41–46). Pittsburgh: Association for Computational Linguistics.

Pearce, D. (2002). A comparative evaluation of collocation extraction techniques. In *Proceedings of the Third International Conference on Language Resources and Evaluation (LREC'02). Las Palmas: European language resources association* (pp. 1530–1536). http://www.lrec-conf.org/proceedings/lrec2002/pdf/169.pdf.

Pecina, P. (2005). An extensive empirical study of collocation extraction methods. In *Proceedings of the ACL student research workshop* (pp. 13–18). Ann Arbor: Association for Computational Linguistic http://aclweb.org/anthology/P05-2003.

Pecina, P. (2010). Lexical association measures and collocation extraction. *Language Resources and Evaluation, 44*, 137–158 https://doi.org/10.1007/s10579-009-9101-4.

Pecina, P., & Schlesinger, P. (2006). Combining association measures for collocation extraction. In *Proceedings of the COLING/ACL 2006 main conference poster sessions* (pp. 651–658). Sydney: Association for Computational Linguistics http://aclweb.org/anthology/P06-2084.

Rodríguez-Fernández, S., Anke, L. E., Carlini, R., & Wanner, L. (2016). Semantics-driven recognition of collocations using word embeddings. In *Proceedings of the 54th annual meeting of the Association for Computational Linguistics (Volume 2: Short Papers)* (pp. 499–505). Berlin: Association for Computational Linguistics https://doi.org/10.18653/v1/P16-2081.

Sangati, F., & van Cranenburgh, A. (2015). Multiword expression identification with recurring tree fragments and association measures. In *Proceedings of the 11th workshop on multiword expressions* (pp. 10–18). Denver: Association for Computational Linguistics https://doi.org/10.3115/v1/W15-0902.

Schäfer, R. (2015). Processing and querying large web corpora with the COW14 architecture. In P. Bański, H. Biber, E. Breiteneder, M. Kupietz, H. Lüngen, & A. Witt (Eds.), *Proceedings of the 3rd workshop on challenges in the Management of Large Corpora (CMLC-3)* (pp. 28–34). Mannheim: IDS Publication Server https://ids-pub.bsz-bw.de/files/3826/Schaefer_Processing_and_querying_large_web_corpora_2015.pdf.

Schäfer, R., & Bildhauer, F. (2012). Building large corpora from the web using a new efficient tool chain. In N. Calzolari, K. Choukri, T. Declerck, M. U. Doğan, B. Maegaard, J. Mariani, A. Moreno, J. Odijk, & S. Piperidis (Eds.), *Proceedings of the eighth international conference on language resources and evaluation (LREC'12)* (pp. 486–493). Istanbul: European Language Resources Association http://www.lrec-conf.org/proceedings/lrec2012/pdf/834_Paper.pdf.

Schulte im Walde, S. (2003). A collocation database for German verbs and nouns. In *Proceedings of the 7th conference on computational lexicography and text research (COMPLEX'03)* (pp. 73–81). Budapest.: http://www.ims.uni-stuttgart.de/institut/mitarbeiter/schulte/publications/workshop/complex-03.pdf.

Schuster, S., & Manning, C. D. (2016). Enhanced English universal dependencies: An improved representation for natural language understanding tasks. In N. Calzolari, K. Choukri, T. Declerck, S. Goggi, M. Grobelnik, B. Maegaard, J. Mariani, H. Mazo, A. Moreno, J. Odijk, & S. Piperidis (Eds.), *Proceedings of the tenth international conference on language resources and evaluation (LREC'16)* (pp. 2371–2378). Portorož: European Language Resources Association http://www.lrec-conf.org/proceedings/lrec2016/pdf/779_Paper.pdf.

Seretan, V. (2008). *Collocation extraction based on syntactic parsing*. Ph.D. thesis, Faculté des lettres, Université de Genève http://www.issco.unige.ch/en/staff/seretan/publ/PhDThesis-VioletaSeretan.pdf.

Seretan, V., & Wehrli, E. (2006). Accurate collocation extraction using a multilingual parser. In *Proceedings of the 21st international conference on computational linguistics and 44th annual meeting of the Association for Computational Linguistics* (pp. 953–960). Sydney: Association for Computational Linguistics http://aclweb.org/anthology/P06-1120.

Seretan, V., Nerima, L., & Wehrli, E. (2003). Extraction of multi-word collocations using syntactic bigram composition. In *Proceedings of the fourth international conference on recent advances in NLP (RANLP-2003)* (pp. 424–431). https://archive-ouverte.unige.ch/unige:17034.

Seretan, V., Nerima, L., & Wehrli, E. (2004). Multi-word collocation extraction by syntactic composition of collocation bigrams. In N. Nicolov, K. Bontcheva, G. Angelova, & R. Mitkov (Eds.), *Recent advances in natural language processing III. Selected papers from RANLP 2003* (pp. 91–100). Amsterdam/Philadelphia: John Benjamins https://doi.org/10.1075/cilt.260.10ser.

Squillante, L. (2014). Towards an empirical subcategorization of multiword expressions. In *Proceedings of the 10th workshop on multiword expressions (MWE 2014)* (pp. 77–81). Gothenburg: Association for Computational Linguistics http://www.aclweb.org/anthology/W14-0813.

Steedman, M. (2000). *The syntactic process*. Cambridge, MA: The MIT Press.

Stefanowitsch, A., & Gries, S. T. (2005). Covarying collexemes. *Corpus Linguistics and Linguistic Theory, 1*(1), 1–43. https://doi.org/10.1515/cllt.2005.1.1.1.

Stefanowitsch, A., & Gries, S. T. (2009). Corpora and grammar. In A. Lüdeling & M. Kytö (Eds.), *Corpus linguistics: An international handbook* (Vol. 2, pp. 933–952). Berlin, DE/New York, NY: Walter de Gruyter.

Teufel, S., & Grefenstette, G. (1995). Corpus-based method for automatic identification of support verbs for nominalizations. In *Proceedings of the seventh conference of the European chapter of the Association for Computational Linguistics (EACL'95)* (pp. 98–103). Dublin: Association for Computational Linguistics http://aclweb.org/anthology/E95-1014.

Tsvetkov, Y., & Wintner, S. (2014). Identification of multiword expressions by combining multiple linguistic information sources. *Computational Linguistics, 40*(2), 449–468 https://doi.org/10.1162/COLI_a_00177.

Uhrig, P., & Proisl, T. (2012). Less hay, more needles – Using dependency-annotated corpora to provide lexicographers with more accurate lists of collocation candidates. *Lexicographica, 28*, 141–180 https://doi.org/10.1515/lexi.2012-0009.
Villada, M., & Begoña, M. (2005). *Data-driven identification of fixed expressions and their modifiability*. Ph.D. thesis, University of Groningen http://www.rug.nl/research/portal/files/9790774/thesis.pdf.
Weller, M., & Heid, U. (2010). Extraction of German multiword expressions from parsed corpora using context features. In N. Calzolari, K. Choukri, B. Maegaard, J. Mariani, J. Odijk, S. Piperidis, M. Rosner, & D. Tapias (Eds.), *Proceedings of the seventh international conference on language resources and evaluation (LREC'10)* (pp. 3195–3201). Valletta: European Language Resources Association http://lrec-conf.org/proceedings/lrec2010/pdf/428_Paper.pdf.
Wermter, J., & Hahn, U. (2006). You can't beat frequency (unless you use linguistic knowledge) – A qualitative evaluation of association measures for collocation and term extraction. In *Proceedings of the 21st international conference on computational linguistics and 44th annual meeting of the ACL (ACL'06)* (pp. 785–792). Sydney: Association for Computational Linguistics http://aclweb.org/anthology/P06-1099.
Wiechmann, D. (2008). On the computation of collostruction strength: Testing measures of association as expressions of lexical bias. *Corpus Linguistics and Linguistic Theory, 4*(2), 253–290 https://doi.org/10.1515/CLLT.2008.011.
Yazdani, M., Farahmand, M., & Henderson, J. (2015). Learning semantic composition to detect non-compositionality of multiword expressions. In *Proceedings of the 2015 conference on empirical methods in natural language processing (EMNLP'15)* (pp. 1733–1742). Lisbon: Association for Computational Linguistics http://www.aclweb.org/anthology/D15-1201.
Zinsmeister, H., & Heid, U. (2003). Significant triples: Adjective+noun+verb combinations. In *Proceedings of the 7th conference on computational lexicography and text research (complex 2003)*. Budapest.: http://www.ims.uni-stuttgart.de/%7Ezinsmeis/pubs/SigColl-paper.pdf.
Zinsmeister, H., & Heid, U. (2004). Collocations of complex nouns: Evidence for lexicalisation. In *Proceedings of KONVENS 2004*. Vienna.: https://pdfs.semanticscholar.org/3e5d/d62cbe41b8aa4bbdf37231b85b9b7ef7d94e.pdf.

Dictionaries

OALD8 = *Oxford Advanced Learner's Dictionary of Current English*, 8th edition (2010). Edited by Joanna Turnbull. Oxford: Oxford University Press.
OCD2 = *Oxford Collocations Dictionary for Students of English*, 2nd edition (2009). Edited by Colin MacIntosh. Oxford: Oxford University Press.

The manufacturer's authorised representative in the EU is Springer Nature Customer Service Centre GmbH, Europaplatz 3, 69115 Heidelberg, Germany. If you have any concerns regarding our products, please contact ProductSafety@springernature.com

Printed and bound by CPI Group (UK) Ltd, Croydon, CR0 4YY
05/10/2026
02228152-0009